SELF-PUBLISHING SIMPLIFIED

A COMPREHENSIVE GUIDE TO PRODUCING, LAUNCHING, AND MARKETING A PROFITABLE BOOK

KRISTEN KIEFFER

Self-Publishing Simplified: A Comprehensive Guide to Producing, Launching, and Marketing a Profitable Book

First Edition (2022).

The advice shared in this book is based on the author's personal experience as an independent author and writing coach. Please apply the advice herein to your book publication and marketing plans at your discretion.

ISBN: 978-1-7342064-4-9

Published by She's Novel Press.

Cover design by Kristen Kieffer

Cover computer icon by Freepik

Editing by Sara Letourneau and Sarah Kolb-Williams

CONTENTS

INTRODUCTION

For many writers, the prospect of producing, self-publishing, and marketing a profitable book poses an intimidating learning curve—a veritable Mount Everest of creative feats. Nevertheless, this endeavor is one that many writers must face to transform their writing dreams into reality. Do you find yourself in this situation, writer?

Perhaps you're interested in self-publishing your debut book, but you have no idea where to begin. You've researched the process online, but the how-to guides and articles you find leave you feeling overwhelmed rather than empowered. You're not sure how to hire a freelance editor or commission a cover design. You're confused by terms like *distributor*, *aggregator*, and *print-on-demand*, and the "going wide versus staying exclusive" conversation has tempted you to chuck your manuscript out the window rather than move forward with self-publishing. You're desperate for clear, comprehensive guidance, and you're hoping this book will prove the perfect resource.

Or maybe you're not yet sure which publishing path you'd like to pursue. Some aspects of the traditional publishing industry appeal to you, especially the possibility of making it big as a world-renowned author. But part of you also longs to forgo industry gatekeepers and rejection in favor of taking full control of your publishing experience. You're torn, so you'd like to learn all you can about both of these publishing options to determine which path is right for you. Thus, you've picked up this book.

There's also the chance that you've already self-published a book, but you regret some of the choices you made the first time around. Maybe you uploaded your manuscript to Amazon without having it professionally edited, and now your listing features several one- and two-star reviews. Maybe you designed your book cover using a free online app, and you're worried that the amateur cover is the reason you haven't sold any books. Or maybe you self-published cheaply for the experience, and now you're ready to get serious about making a profit with your creative work. Regardless, you're eager to level up your self-publishing knowledge before producing and launching your next book, and you're hoping this guide can help.

Whatever the case, you're now staring at the self-publishing learning curve with one all-important question in mind: *How do I make the climb?* Every late-night Google search has left you with more questions than answers, and you're worried that your writing dreams will remain forever out of reach.

I hear you, writer. I know what you're experiencing—the fear, the yearning, the overwhelm. I know because I've been there myself.

In 2015, I started a blog called She's Novel to document everything I learned about storytelling as I wrote my debut novel. To my surprise, the blog attracted a notable following. I monetized the site by engaging in affiliate opportunities and selling digital workbooks that transformed storytelling principles into actionable writing exercises. Within two years, my budding online business proved profitable enough that I quit my day job, relaunched my website as Well-Storied, and started earning a living as a full-time creative entrepreneur. It was an exciting transition, but I felt like something was missing. There was a hole in my creative work that left me feeling vaguely hollow. Another two years passed before I finally understood what that something was: authorship.

For all my creative success, I hadn't pursued my lifelong dream of publishing a book. Instead, I'd let my novels and nonfiction book ideas take the back burner to simpler digital products I was selling directly through my website. A daunting dose of introspection revealed a lack of confidence in my ability to self-publish. The process was too complicated, I'd told myself. It was reserved for writers who had more ambition and initiative than me.

It was a limiting belief I could no longer abide by.

Throughout 2019, I worked feverishly to draft, revise, and produce my first nonfiction book, a self-development guide for authors called *Build Your Best Writing Life*. I self-published the book on January 2, 2020, and the book launch strategies I put into practice proved successful. During its first week in the world, *Build Your Best Writing Life* sold over 400 copies and rose among my chosen Amazon categories to rank alongside books like *On Writing* by Stephen King and Strunk and White's *The Elements of Style*. The book has since received dozens of rave reviews and over 100 five-star ratings on Amazon—and it has earned me a nice chunk of change along the way.

Successfully self-publishing a book filled the hole in my creative spirit and left me feeling profoundly proud of my efforts. But there was a dark side to my first self-publishing experience: nothing—and I mean *nothing*—about self-publishing *Build Your Best Writing Life* was easy.

Before producing the book, I spent months scouring the internet for answers to my myriad questions about self-publishing. Some resources provided insight into one or two key aspects of the process, but I consistently spent just as much time seeking helpful resources as I did absorbing them. It was an inefficient, mentally exhausting affair that forced me to slowly cobble together the strategies and know-how I needed to successfully produce, publish, and market my first book. All the while, I knew there had to be a better way—a simple, actionable resource that could guide writers through the process of self-publishing a profitable book.

Acclaimed American author Toni Morrison once said, "If you find a book you really want to read but it hasn't been written yet, then you must write it." Thus, *Self-Publishing Simplified* was born.

The book you now hold in your hands compiles all the information I desperately needed when preparing to publish *Build Your Best Writing Life*. It's a comprehensive starter guide to self-publishing a profitable book with confidence and clarity. To help you through each stage of the process, I've divided this book into three sections.

In part 1, you'll learn everything you need to know *before* setting out on your self-publishing journey. You'll discover the pros and cons of self-publishing and determine your personal definition of publishing success. You'll familiarize yourself with the cost of producing a high-quality book and how **independent authors** (i.e., authors who self-publish professionally; indie authors) earn their livings. Finally, you'll explore the roles that your creative niche and your mindset play in achieving success as a self-published author.

Part 2 offers a detailed look at the process of producing and self-publishing a book. You'll learn how to work with freelance editors to polish your manuscript, as well as how to commission cover designs and format your book for sale. You'll explore various book distribution options, craft listings that boost your book's visibility in online marketplaces, and tap into the fastest growing area of the book industry by learning how to produce an audiobook.

In part 3, you'll dive into the business side of self-publishing by learning how to successfully market your published book. First, you'll establish your **author platform** (i.e., the visibility and credibility that will help you reach readers and sell more books). Then you'll explore the five main types of book marketing: content marketing, email marketing, paid advertising, visibility marketing, and spike marketing. Finally, you'll learn how to implement these strategies for lucrative, fulfilling, sustainable indie author success.

By the time you finish reading *Self-Publishing Simplified*, you'll have all the vital information you need to produce, publish, and market your novel, memoir, or nonfiction book. You can then use this book as a reference guide, returning to applicable chapters at each stage of your self-publishing journey.

However, before you dive in, there's an important truth you must accept: Self-publishing isn't easy—at least not the first time around.

This book will simplify the self-publishing process by offering valuable insights and actionable advice, but it won't flatten the learning curve you're facing. You'll still need to strap on your own gear and make the climb. My hope is to ease your journey by serving as your creative Sherpa, leading you across treacherous self-publishing terrain and telling you where to put your toes as you launch and market your book.

Does this analogy seem silly to you? I don't use it lightly.

In many ways, self-publishing a profitable book is as difficult and exhilarating as any epic travel adventure. If summiting Mount Everest isn't your style, insert your adventure of choice. Hike the Appalachian Trail, cycle to Patagonia, or backpack across Europe. My point is this: Thousands of people long to go on epic travel adventures, yet few ever step beyond the borders of their hometowns. Fear of the unknown keeps them rooted, safe but unsatisfied. Many justify their inaction with excuses such as "One day, when I retire . . ." or "If only things were different . . ."

Writer, I want you to know that you're capable of climbing the self-publishing learning curve. Not *one day*, and not *if only*. If you're passionate about your creative work and energized by the idea of making a profit as a published author, the time to kick-start your self-publishing journey has arrived. Are you brave enough to step outside your comfort zone? To strap on your climbing gear and get to work? Then let's get started.

PART I

THE FOUNDATIONS OF SUCCESSFUL SELF-PUBLISHING

1

IS SELF-PUBLISHING RIGHT FOR YOU?

Before embarking on your self-publishing journey, it's important to consider whether publishing independently is truly the best option for you and your books.

Many writers view self-publishing as the backup plan they'll pursue if they can't secure a literary agent or book deal in the traditional publishing industry. But those who treat self-publishing as a secondary plan in case of industry rejection may be setting themselves up for a rude awakening. Self-publishing isn't an easy alternative to traditional publishing. It's a valid publication path that has its own challenges and essential knowledge, and none of that should be taken lightly. With that in mind, which publication path is right for you? To answer this question, you'll first need to understand the options available to you.

Traditionally, an author sells their manuscript's publication rights to a publishing house in exchange for contracted terms of payment. The publisher produces and distributes the author's book to retailers, then pays the author for books sold according to the contracted terms.

Most book deals include two primary forms of payment:

royalties and an advance. A **royalty** is the sum of money an author earns for each sale of their book, which is determined by contracted royalty rates (e.g., 25 percent of list price per unit sold). Most book deals include individual royalty rates for each edition of a book the publisher plans to produce, such as hardcover, paperback, and e-book. However, most traditionally published authors don't earn royalties immediately after their books are published. Instead, an author must first earn out their **advance**, which is the set sum of money they're paid (often in multiple installments) leading up to their book's publication. An author is guaranteed to earn their advance regardless of how well their book sells, but they won't earn royalties until they've sold enough copies to recoup their advance. For example, let's say an author signs a book deal with a $10,000 advance and 10 percent royalty rates on sales of all editions. Under these conditions, their book would need to earn $100,000 in revenue—recouping their original $10,000 advance at 10 percent—before they would begin receiving royalty payments.

Independent authors take a different approach to publishing their books. Instead of selling their manuscript's publication rights to a publishing house, an indie author retains those rights and finances their book's production and distribution out of pocket. Most indie authors work directly with online book retailers and distributors to list their books for sale in online marketplaces. They then earn royalties in the same way as traditionally published authors, though they're paid by the distributors through which they've listed their book rather than by a publishing house.

In taking this approach, indie authors reap a host of benefits that can make self-publishing a lucrative, fulfilling endeavor. But publishing independently also comes at a cost— literally and figuratively. To ensure that you choose the right

publication path for you and your books, let's take a closer look at self-publishing's advantages and disadvantages.

The Advantages of Indie Authorship

The reasons one writer may have for choosing to publish independently are often the same reasons another writer may have for deciding on traditional publishing. Nevertheless, let's look at six common reasons why many writers are attracted to the idea of publishing independently.

Reason 1: Indie Authors Maintain Creative Control

Authors who self-publish always maintain full creative control over their book's content and presentation. This isn't the case for traditionally published authors, who are largely beholden to their publishers' whims. While most publishers strive to honor their authors' creative visions, their primary concern is ultimately their bottom line. Many traditionally published authors have had to begrudgingly accept book titles, cover designs, and even major rewrites to avoid risking a breach of contract or their publishers' willingness to offer additional book deals.

Reason 2: Indie Authors Earn More Money per Book

Indie authors benefit from higher royalty rates and more frequent payouts than their traditionally published counterparts. Most traditional royalty rates fall between 15 and 25 percent, and traditionally published authors are typically paid only twice a year. Moreover, traditionally published authors only earn royalties after they earn out their advances—and even then, they have to pay their agents an industry-standard 15 percent cut before their income hits their bank accounts. Indie authors, on the other hand, frequently enjoy 60 to 80 percent royalty rates and are paid monthly.

Reason 3: Indie Authors Can Publish Their Books Much Sooner

If you think six months between paychecks is a long time, you may find the traditional publishing timeline even more frightening. Most traditionally published books don't hit shelves for two or more years *after* authors sign their book deals. And that's not counting the time these authors spend landing a literary agent and then a publishing contract. Altogether it's a significant time to wait to see one's book on shelves.

Indie authors, however, enjoy a much faster publishing timeline. While the production process (i.e., freelance editing, cover design, formatting) may take several months, listing a book for sale online can take as little as twenty-four hours. Incredible, right?

Reason 4: Indie Authors Avoid Rejection from Industry Gatekeepers

What indie authors save in time, they also save in emotional turmoil. Most traditionally published authors experience months—if not years—of silence and rejection as they query literary agents. Then they experience more of the same as their literary agents shop their manuscripts around to publishers. This process of appeasing industry gatekeepers can be demoralizing, to say the least. And for many writers, the repeated rejection can weigh heavily on their limiting beliefs, causing more emotional distress than they'd care to admit.

Self-published authors, on the other hand, are fortunate enough to escape this fate. They can publish whatever they want, whenever they'd like. No questions asked. No rejection.

Reason 5: Indie Authors Typically Avoid Rejection over the Long Term

For traditionally published authors, the unfortunate likelihood of emotional distress doesn't dissipate after they sign on the dotted line. One signed book deal is no guarantee of an ongoing relationship with their literary agent or publisher, especially if their published book undersells. So, after spending years trying to break into the industry, traditionally published authors may sometimes find themselves starting from scratch, wondering once more whether their work will ever be good enough to please industry gatekeepers.

Thankfully, indie authors don't have to endure this kind of uncertainty. While building a career as a self-published author can be unpredictable in its own way, indie authors enjoy far more agency over the future of their careers—and they never have to fear being rejected even after they've gotten their careers off the ground.

Reason 6: Indie Authors Retain Control of Their Books' Publication Rights

When an author inks a traditional book deal, they sell their manuscript's publication rights to their publisher for a set amount of time. This exchange isn't without risk. Certain circumstances can leave a contract in limbo with the book unpublished and the author unable to regain the right to seek publication elsewhere for several months—or even years.

Fortunately, self-published authors don't have to worry whether an **acquisitions editor** (i.e., an editor responsible for acquiring marketable books for a publishing house) will quit or whether their **imprint** (i.e., the brand name under which a book is published) will fold. Instead, they retain full control of their books' publication rights at all times, no matter where they choose to publish online.

The Disadvantages of Publishing Independently

Despite its many exciting benefits, self-publishing won't be the right publication path for every writer—maybe even you. That's why it's important to discuss the six most common reasons why authors choose to publish traditionally instead.

Reason 1: Indie Authors Must Make a Financial Investment When Self-Publishing

When an author publishes traditionally, their publisher foots all of the expenses required to produce their book. This includes everything from paying freelance editors, cover designers, and book formatters to purchasing **ISBNs** (i.e., International Standard Book Numbers) and paying for printing. Indie authors don't have this benefit. Instead, every dollar required to produce a self-published book must come out of the author's pocket.

Technically, it's possible to self-publish a book on the cheap or even for free, but producing a well-designed, professionally edited book that readers will want to read requires an up-front investment. Most indie authors spend at least $1,000—and often between $2,500 and $5,000—to produce every book they write with no guarantee that they'll ever earn that money back.

Reason 2: Indie Authors Must Be Their Own Project Managers

The expense of hiring freelance editors, cover designers, and other publishing team members isn't the only added responsibility that indie authors must shoulder. The process of building a publishing team can be a lot to manage in and of itself. While many indie authors enjoy the freedom of choosing who will work on their books, the reality is that finding reputable creatives who work within your genre, offer services that fit your budget, and have availability in their schedules to take on your project can be difficult. The host of poorly trained freelancers and questionable companies that loudly tout their services online can complicate your effort to build the right publishing team for you and your book.

Reason 3: Indie Authors Must Act as Business Owners

Hiring professional services is just one of the responsibilities that prove how independent publishing is an entrepreneurial act. An author's books are their products, their readers are their customers, and every aspect of running their businesses—from business planning to product design, bookkeeping, and beyond —is their responsibility.

Traditionally published authors also need to act as entrepreneurs in some respects. As neither employees nor independent contractors, they operate as self-employed creators who license their **intellectual property** (i.e., creative work protected under law from unauthorized use) to publishers. But many of the responsibilities authors face are mitigated by the help of a literary agent and publisher. Without similar support, an indie author may struggle to get their business—in other words, their writing career—off the ground.

Reason 4: Indie Authors Have Limited Access to External Rewards

Indie authors must accept that they're unlikely to achieve many of the more publicly gratifying forms of authorial success: book tours, best-seller lists, literary awards, and film adaptations, to name a few. While these achievements are technically available to self-published authors, most are improbable—even more so than they are for traditionally published authors. Only the most critically or commercially successful authors are likely to attain these rewards, and most require the backing of a powerful publishing house. For indie authors, success typically has more to do with financial stability and happy readers than with public renown.

Reason 5: Indie Authors Have Less Control over Their Books' Visibility

Speaking of success, rising through the sales ranks in popular online book marketplaces can be more difficult for self-published authors. Traditionally published authors benefit from their publisher's ability to actively position promising books as visibly as possible online and in stores, paying for placements that simply aren't available to indie authors. While self-published authors can tailor their book's metadata for visibility, where their book is "shelved" online is largely determined by algorithms that rely on sales figures, ratings, and author rank—all of which debut authors lack.

Fortunately, indie authors can use other marketing tactics to help their debut books rise through the ranks. (We'll talk more about book launch strategies in chapter 20.) But ultimately, indie authors are at a distinct disadvantage when it comes to ensuring their books' visibility in oversaturated online markets.

Reason 6: Indie Authors Are More Susceptible to Self-Publishing Stigma

Finally, let's not forget the elephant in the room: self-publishing stigma. The belief that self-published books are poorly written and therefore lesser than their traditional counterparts is fading by the year. Still, self-published authors continue to face stigma concerning the quality and legitimacy of their work. This stigma is rarely an overwhelming obstacle, but the limiting beliefs triggered by self-publishing stigma can be easy to internalize. For some indie authors, the fact that they chose to forgo traditional publishing can ultimately lead them to wonder whether they're really a "good enough" writer, no matter how fantastic their published books may be.

The Truth about Book Marketing

Hopefully, reading through the pros and cons of self-publishing has given you a better idea of whether publishing independently is right for you. However, you might be wondering why I didn't mention book marketing as one of the added responsibilities that self-published authors must accept. Don't traditionally published authors benefit from all the book marketing support their publishers provide?

The hard truth of the matter is that all authors, regardless of which publishing path they pursue, must do the bulk of their own book marketing.

Yes, traditional publishing houses have marketing departments that promote upcoming releases. But traditional book marketing tactics are expensive, and publishers frequently reserve the bulk of their marketing budgets for highly anticipated releases from big-name authors and buzzworthy debuts. The publishers' other authors often have to shoulder the burden of marketing their books on their dime and time, often with very little support. That's why you still see traditionally published authors maintaining their social media accounts, sending newsletters to their readers, and creating book-related merchandise to offer their audiences. Never mind those that promote their work via book tours, literary conferences, and industry networking events.

Simply put, book marketing is an essential authorial task no matter which publishing path you pursue. Thankfully, effective book marketing doesn't have to be as time-consuming or soul-sucking as most writers assume. For now, if you aren't willing to spend the time and effort to promote your books, then pursuing a career (or side hustle) as an author likely isn't the right choice for you. Still, that doesn't mean you can't self-publish your books purely for personal fulfillment—which leads us to the most important question you'll need to ask before committing to a publishing path.

2

WHAT IS YOUR PERSONAL DEFINITION OF PUBLISHING SUCCESS?

It's my strong belief that there is no wrong way to be a writer. There is no version of the writing life within ethical reason that's more real or commendable than another. That's true whether you write literary novels, Harlequin romance, heavily researched popular science tomes, or memoirs from personal experience. All writing is an art form. All writing has its place.

By extension, I believe in the validity of every legitimate path to publication. I believe in the necessity of the traditional publishing industry just as I believe in the power of independent publishing. I also reject the patronizing stigma that punishes self-published authors, and I praise writers who choose to forgo professional publishing altogether in favor of more personal forms of creative fulfillment.

At the end of the day, the only "right" way to be a writer is to create with unabashed joy. Nothing more, and nothing less. Fan fiction, journal scribbles, Instagram poetry, travel blogging—it's all as remarkable and legitimate a form of creation as any *New York Times* best seller or six-figure **backlist** (i.e., the extent of an author's published books available for sale). The trick, of course, is to discover the paths that awaken your true creative calling.

The Many Paths to Personal Creative Success

Writers and storytellers often pursue publication in search of validation. Society has taught creatives that their work isn't legitimate until it can be commodified and that earning a living with their art is the only way to prove to the world that their art is worthy—and more than just a waste of time.

Writer, please know that this dangerous social narrative is nonsense. You don't become a "real" writer when you sign a book deal or earn your first royalty check. You become a writer the moment you put pen to paper, fingers to keys, or voice to dictation. In other words, you become a writer when you write. Moreover, the time you spend writing is never wasted. To create is an integral part of what it means to be human, and don't you dare let anyone tell you otherwise. Your writing matters.

Even if you write for your eyes only.

Even if you share your work for free online.

Even if you never make a dime.

Your writing matters.

Should the day come when you choose to publish (as it likely has, since you picked up this book), then know that publishing success is a personal pursuit. You alone get to decide what you want to achieve on your publishing journey.

For some, publishing success looks like building a career as a traditionally published author who travels the world to meet fans of their best-selling book series. For others, success is finding financial stability as an independent author. Success can also be a creative entrepreneur cultivating a backlist of self-published books to establish credibility in their field, a tough-as-nails cancer survivor launching a memoir to kick-start their career as an inspirational speaker, or a stay-at-home dad self-publishing wacky alien space thrillers to pad out his children's college fund.

Do you see how there's no lesser way to be an author?

Do you see all the glorious paths one can take to personal publishing success?

As a creative, you get to decide what publishing success means to you. So tell me, writer: What do you want from your publishing experience? Do you want to publish for profit? Do you want to write full-time? What do you hope to accomplish by publishing your creative work?

Now's the time to be brutally honest with yourself. Do you want to hit the *New York Times* best-seller list and become a household name in writing? See your book series adapted for film or television? Build a creative career that allows you to travel full-time? Do you want to monetize the story you've been posting online for free, produce physical copies of the middle-grade books you've been writing for your grandchildren, or cultivate a side hustle that allows you to tap into your banked creativity? Or something else entirely?

Take some time now to write down your creative vision. Put every hope and dream on the page. Dare to think big. Then, when you're done, take a step back. Resist the urge to flip to the next chapter, thinking your work here is done. Before you stake a claim to your creative vision, there's a pivotal aspect of success we must discuss—an aspect that may hold unhealthy sway over your personal definition of publishing success.

Resisting the Persistent Pull of the Ego

If you're like many writers, you may be interested in making it big. You not only want to build a full-time career as a published author, but you also want all the thrilling achievements that come with high-level creative success: best-sellers lists, book tours, film adaptations, and six-figure book deals. Maybe even a literary award or two while you're at it.

There's nothing wrong with desiring this level of success in your writing life. It's only natural to want to leave your mark on the world in a big way. But if your definition of success hinges upon attaining flashy awards and accolades, then here's a hard truth you must accept: You might be setting yourself up for failure.

Hard work and determination can take you far in your creative career. Lucky breaks—and the roads they pave to high-level success—are often found at the intersection of hard work and opportunity. But the reality of any traditional creative industry is that opportunity is limited. There are only so many spots on a best-seller list. There's only so much room in a publisher's budget to coordinate overseas book tours. And only a limited number of optioned books ever receive the full Hollywood treatment. No matter how hard you work, how many connections you make, and how long you keep your nose to the grindstone, these opportunities are largely beyond your control to attain. The chances of rocketing to the same level of stardom as Stephen King, J. K. Rowling, or Nora Roberts are slim to none.

My mission in telling you this isn't to discourage you from dreaming big. By all means, don't make yourself small for the sake of hard truths. Rather, my mission is to ensure that you dream big while keeping your feet firmly planted on the ground, recognizing that true creative joy comes from the foundational work of *creating* rather than *achieving*.

The reason so many writers crave high-level success is because, deep down, they desperately crave creative validation. They need someone to tell them that their work is good enough, that all the time and effort they've poured into their art hasn't been wasted. They crave the reassurance that their work matters and is worthy of taking up space in this world. *If I can make it big,* they think, *then I'll know I'm not some wannabe. I'll know I'm a real writer.*

Notice that all of these needs stem from a place of fear—the need to assuage the worry that one's work *isn't* good enough, that their time and effort *has* been wasted. It comes from the belief that one's work is worthless and embarrassing and should be hidden from the world until someone important deigns to validate its worth. Do you relate to any of these fears, writer? If so, then know this: fear is just your ego talking.

Your ego is your sense of self-worth and esteem. It's your belief in your own value and importance. Unfortunately, the default state of the human ego is troublingly fragile. Rather than recognizing its worth as innate, the unchecked ego seeks proof in the form of external validation. It craves acceptance from authority figures and the "cool crowd"—the people it both admires and envies. For writers, ego often manifests as a desperate need to please critics and industry gatekeepers. It makes authors believe that if they make it big, they'll have proof that they're good enough and that they're real writers. But the ego's fatal flaw lies in its fear.

If you fail to check your ego, then no great height will ever be enough. Should you land a book deal, your ego will remind you that you can't quit your day job yet. Should you hit a best-seller list, your ego will whisper that there's no guarantee your next book will find similar success. Should your book be optioned for television, your ego will quake with the possibility that readers will hate the show and your subsequent book sales will tank. And on and on and on it will go.

As you consider your personal definition of publishing success, take a moment to address your ego. Listen to its fears, and acknowledge the role it plays in your desires. This is vulnerable work, and giving voice to your ego can be painful. But if you fail to brave your ego, then you'll always keep yourself small, scared, and unsatisfied, no matter how big you make it as an author. That's no way to live, writer. You deserve to create boldly and proudly in all the incredible ways that bring you joy. Will you choose that for yourself?

In *Build Your Best Writing Life*, I shared how writers can brave the pull of resistance in their writing lives and how they can confront the ego-driven fears and limiting beliefs that keep them from creating with confidence and assurance. If this topic resonates with you, give that book a read. But for now, simply know that you're enough. You're a real writer because you write. Your work matters because it brings you joy, hope, or healing—and it holds the power to do the same for thousands of readers around the world.

So go ahead and dream big. Ambition is far from a dirty word. But consider whether the ego is making an appearance in your creative vision. Is your definition of success marred by an unhealthy desire for external validation or public praise? Take a moment to review your definition of publishing success. Why did you define success the way you did? Why do you want to achieve it? How will it benefit your life? Why does it matter to you?

Most of your wildest writing dreams are unlikely realities, and that's OK. There's nothing wrong with chasing them for the sake of sheer excitement. But don't allow awards and accolades to determine the fulfillment you find in your creative career. Instead, treat high-level achievements as happy by-products of a privileged writing life. View them as unexpected highlights on a journey you already love with your whole heart—a journey you'll continue to undertake even if no such success ever comes your way because you know beyond a shadow of a doubt that every step is worth just as much as the destination you aim to reach.

Defining a Healthy View of Publishing Success

If all my waxing poetic has led you to wonder what a healthy definition of publishing success actually looks like, then let's break this concept down together.

Every author's definition of publishing success will be unique, but a healthy creative vision is always rooted in metrics that are largely within your realm of control. In other words, it's rooted in strong possibilities rather than unlikely realities. It's OK if some lucky breaks are necessary so long as patience and persistence still pave the way. For example, there's no guarantee that you'll ever make a living as an indie author. However, there's a good chance that you'll succeed if you keep building your backlist, developing your platform, and actively working to get your books into readers' hands. The same goes for traditional publishing. Whether a literary agent or publisher will sign your work is outside your control, but persistently crafting and pitching high-quality books is likely to lead to a book deal in due course.

As you work to identify your definition of publishing success, you may find it helpful to ask the following questions:

1. Why Do I Want to Publish My Books?

Why is it important for you to share your creative work with the world? What do you hope to achieve by publishing your books? Do you want to entertain readers as you've been entertained? Inspire those who are experiencing a personal struggle you've overcome? Do you want to teach readers how to get started in your favorite hobby, infuse your favorite genre with a fresh perspective, or prove to your kids that it's never too late to chase their dreams? The possibilities are endless, writer.

2. What Do I Hope to Achieve as a Published Author?

What are your goals for your publishing experience? Do you want to write and share all of the books in your epic fantasy series? Publish one new romance novel a year? How about build credibility for your spiritual wellness business? Or develop a middle-grade series that helps you connect with kids during speaking events in your local community? Don't be afraid to think outside the box. This is your writing life. Spend it creating in all of the ways that bring you joy.

3. Do I Want to Publish for Profit?

Be honest with yourself. It's OK if you'd prefer to keep your creative work a hobby. If you do want to publish for profit, what level of income do you hope to achieve? If you want to write full-time, how much money will you need to make to cover your expenses? To live your ideal lifestyle and save for the future? Be as specific as possible when answering these questions. The better you understand your budget and financial goals, the clearer your monetary metrics for success will be.

Determine Your Publishing Path

With a clear definition of personal publishing success in place, it's time to reevaluate whether self-publishing is right for you. Consider the pros and cons that were addressed during chapter 1. Will the benefits of self-publishing help you achieve your unique definition of publishing success? Are you willing to sacrifice the advantages of publishing traditionally in favor of sharing your books with the world as an independent author?

If you aren't sure which path is right for you, know that you don't have to make an either-or decision. Hybrid authors publish both traditionally *and* independently. Fantasy writing duo Ilona and Andrew Gordon, who publish under the pen name Ilona Andrews, are a prime example of successful hybrid authors. Alternatively, some authors transition from one publishing path to another. Talia Hibbert spent years self-publishing popular contemporary romance novels before accepting a book deal for *Get a Life, Chloe Brown* and the subsequent books in her best-selling Brown Sisters series.

Other authors choose to work with **assisted self-publishing companies** (i.e., companies that shoulder the responsibility of producing all aspects of an author's self-published book for an up-front fee), which can mitigate some of the responsibilities that might make an author question whether self-publishing is their best path forward. If you're curious about this route, you'll enjoy the section on assisted self-publishing companies in the next chapter.

All this being said, you might still be having a hard time determining your personal definition of publishing success because you'd like to learn more about the publishing paths available to you. Self-publishing can be an attractive option for many writers, but this route can be difficult to pursue if you can't (or aren't willing to) spend the money to produce high-quality books out of pocket. With that in mind, let's take a closer look at the financial side of self-publishing a book.

3

THE UP-FRONT COST OF SELF-PUBLISHING A BOOK

The freedom to publish whatever you want whenever you'd like makes self-publishing an attractive option for many writers. But this type of creative freedom comes—quite literally—at a cost. Understanding the expenses involved in self-publishing is key to determining whether you want to pursue a career as an independent author. With that in mind, let's answer this all-important question: How much does it cost to self-publish a book?

Here's the simple answer: however much you'd like.

Most **online distributors** (i.e., the platforms that help writers list their books for sale on popular online marketplaces) don't charge writers a fee to list their books. This means that it's entirely possible to self-publish a book without spending a dime, but only if you're willing to skip freelance editing, design your book cover, and format your manuscript using a free do-it-yourself (DIY) option. However, this isn't the wisest course of action if you're hoping to make a living (or, at the very least, a profit) with your published books.

To make a living as an independent author, the books you write and publish must be largely indistinguishable from similar books produced by traditional publishers. There are rarely exceptions to this rule. A DIY clip art book cover simply isn't going to entice readers when it's tucked between listings that feature Fabio-esque models with fabulous hair or stunning pieces of graphic art. Readers are also unlikely to purchase more than one of your books if their first reading experience was riddled with typos or sloppy storytelling.

Readers buy books whose listings speak to the quality of their content. They then continue to buy from authors whose books live up to their expectations. To meet readers' expectations, you need to produce a high-quality book, and no writer can accomplish this task on their own. We're simply too close to our manuscripts and too specialized in our skill sets to excel at every aspect of the book production process, and that's OK. There's a reason traditional publishers assign a team of professionals to every book they produce. If you choose to publish independently, it will be your job to build this professional publishing team for yourself. That's why the vast majority of successful indie authors commission some or all of the following services for each book they publish:

- Developmental editing
- Line editing and copyediting
- Proofreading
- Formatting/interior design
- Cover design

These are the same pre-publication tasks that manuscripts undergo in the hands of a traditional publishing team. The only difference is that indie authors must pay for these services out of pocket. However, the cost of these services can vary wildly depending upon the length and complexity of the manuscript, the difficulty of the work required, and the unique pricing model that each company or freelancer employs. With these factors in mind, most indie authors budget between US $1,000 and $5,000 to produce every book they publish.

Bear in mind that you can find most pre-publication services available online at a wide range of price points. When perusing these services, know that—generally speaking—you get what you pay for. It isn't necessary to employ the most expensive services on the market, especially if they don't fit your budget. However, beware of offers that seem too good (and too cheap) to be true. Plenty of midrange pre-publication services are available online that bridge the gap between quality and affordability. Just be sure to do your research to ensure that these services are reputable and recommended.

In part 2, we'll take a closer look at commissioning each of these pre-publication services. For now, let's explore an overview of the nature and cost of each service. Please note that price ranges included in this chapter are generalizations based on personal experience and research rather than hard data. Your mileage may vary. Please note that all prices are listed in US dollars.

Developmental Editing

Also known as content or structural editors, developmental editors help authors polish the structure and content of their books. A fiction developmental editor addresses a story's plot, character arcs, worldbuilding (if it's speculative fiction), themes, and other foundational story elements. A nonfiction developmental editor evaluates the manuscript's clarity, organization, and effectiveness.

A full developmental edit is highly detailed and includes in-line manuscript notes, making it the most expensive form of freelance editing. More affordable forms of developmental editing include manuscript critiques, evaluations, and editorial letters that provide broader feedback on your story. Authors on tighter budgets may choose to forgo developmental editing, relying instead on unpaid amateur feedback from beta readers or critique partners as they polish their stories for publication.

Depending on the service you commission, developmental editing may range between $500 and $3,500 for a 70,000-word manuscript.

Line Editing and Copyediting

Though line editing may address spelling and grammar errors, its main purpose is to ensure that authors use the best possible language to convey their points or tell their stories. Line editing also helps authors refine their writing styles. Copyediting, on the other hand, focuses on the consistency and accuracy of the language an author uses throughout their manuscript. Think sentence structure, word choice, verb tense, voice, and point of view.

Because line editing and copyediting both address the language used throughout a manuscript, these forms of editing are sometimes conflated. However, many editors offer line editing and copyediting as distinct services.

As its own service, line editing can range between $1,000 and $2,500 for a 70,000-word manuscript, while copyediting often ranges between $500 and $1,500. However, some editors offer bundled line editing and copyediting services at reduced rates. Some also offer general writing style evaluations that are less expensive than traditional line editing or copyediting services.

Proofreading

Though proofreading is often defined as the act of combing through text to find and fix spelling and grammar errors, the true scope of this work is much more detailed. Traditional proofreading takes place *after* a manuscript has been formatted. The work itself consists of ensuring that a **printed** or **digital proof** (i.e., a formatted pre-publication copy of a book) matches the text of the finalized manuscript, contains no remaining errors or inconsistencies, and is formatted correctly for print-on-demand and online distribution.

Some editors conflate copyediting and proofreading services, pitching this work under the label "proofreading." Editors who offer this type of service typically perform their edits on an author's manuscript rather than a formatted proof. This isn't an issue for authors who plan to upload their manuscripts solely for e-book distribution, since most book distributors will convert a basic Microsoft Word document or PDF file into an EPUB file free of charge. However, authors who plan to publish print books or e-books with advanced formatting should seek traditional proofreading to ensure that there are no formatting errors in their proofs.

Traditional proofreading rates can fall anywhere between $200 and $800 for a 75,000-word manuscript depending upon the complexity of the work. Conflated copyediting and proofreading services marketed as "proofreading" typically cost a bit more. However, many editors offer bundled (rather than conflated) copyediting and proofreading services at reduced rates. Keep an eye out for deals.

Formatting/Interior Design

Though once *referred* to as separate pre-publication tasks, both *formatting* and *interior design* now refer to the act of preparing the layout of a manuscript for print and digital distribution.

Because a manuscript must be formatted separately for each edition an author chooses to publish (e.g., paperback, large print, e-book), interior design can quickly become an expensive out-of-pocket cost. The good news is that formatting is the one part of the book production process that many authors can complete themselves without risking an amateur result. Various formatting apps, templates, and DIY tutorials can help authors create beautifully formatted books for a more affordable out-of-pocket expense (or even for free!). That said, DIY book formatting takes time and can be finicky depending on the method used. Therefore, it's common for authors to hire a professional book formatter to complete this task for them.

With this in mind, popular interior design options can range between $0 and $600 depending on the chosen method and the number of editions an author plans to publish. Manuscripts with copious charts, images, or other advanced design needs may cost more to format.

Cover Design

At the end of the day, readers *do* judge books by their covers. Given that a column of covers is the first thing readers see when perusing online book listings, it's no wonder that cover design can make or break an author's sales figures. Readers aren't going to linger on a poor-quality or ineffective cover design when more exciting listings are just a click away.

Fortunately, a good cover doesn't have to break the bank. Most cover design companies and freelancers offer premade e-book covers for less than $100, while print and e-book cover design bundles can make custom cover designs more affordable. Some companies and freelancers even offer bundles that pair custom cover design with interior formatting, audiobook cover design, author branding services, or marketing materials. Keep an eye out for great deals, especially if you're on a budget.

As with formatting, you'll need to commission an individual cover design for each edition of your book. The cost of purchasing or commissioning a cover design can range from $49 to $200 for a premade e-book cover design, $400 to $800 for multiple editions of a custom cover design from a cover design company, or $1,500 and over for a custom cover design from a boutique freelance cover designer.

Other Self-Publishing Costs

In addition to the pre-publication services discussed above, some indie authors choose to invest in any of the following:

- Interior illustrations
- Fantasy map design
- Professional headshots
- Professional blurb copy or blurb editing
- Print books for in-person launch events
- Preorder ads
- Author website domain name and hosting
- Marketing tools, merchandise, and book swag
- Launch party materials

Most of these expenses are far from necessary, but you may wish to consider them as you prepare to produce and share your book with the world.

One additional expense that will prove necessary for many indie authors is the cost of purchasing ISBNs. These are unique identifiers that indie authors are required to assign to most editions of their books (and that traditional publishers also apply to all editions they publish).

We'll talk at length about ISBNs in chapter 12. For now, know that ISBNs can be a significant expense. A single ISBN purchased through Bowker, the official ISBN issuer for the United States and Australia, will cost $100. Fortunately, Bowker also offers ISBN bundles that make individual ISBNs more affordable. That said, some indie authors choose to forgo purchasing ISBNs in favor of using the free identifiers Amazon offers to apply to print books. This option limits the number of income streams an author can generate with their books. Nevertheless, it may be a smart choice for authors on a budget.

If you're feeling intimidated by the thought of researching and commissioning so many services (or if you'd simply like to save yourself a bit of time and effort), then you may want to work with an assisted self-publishing company. Assisted self-publishers are companies that provide in-house pre-publication services and self-publishing assistance for a single up-front fee. Most assisted self-publishers offer packages that range between $2,500 and $5,000 depending on the number of services employed and the complexity of the necessary work.

If you're interested in pursuing this option, then be sure to do your research. Unfortunately, some assisted self-publishing companies operate in an exploitative manner, providing authors with subpar services and poor customer support in exchange for a quick buck. While I won't name the most notorious companies here for legal reasons, I encourage you to review resources such as the Science Fiction and Fantasy Writers of America's Writer Beware database to learn about known disreputable companies before signing any contracts. A quick ask among online indie author forums will also result in a host of anecdotal warnings.

No matter how you approach the pre-publication process, I encourage you to determine a budget before diving in. Be honest with yourself. How much can you reasonably afford to spend on publication expenses? Alternatively, how much will you need to save to afford the services you'd like to commission? Entering the pre-publication process with a clearly defined budget will help you identify the right options for you and your book, avoid overspending on premium services, and have a far more positive—and financially stress-free—publication experience.

4

HOW INDEPENDENT AUTHORS EARN
THEIR LIVINGS

I n the Western world, we've been raised to believe that creative work doesn't pay the bills. Art degrees are useless, creative careers are limited, and only the most brilliant talents succeed at earning a living with their art—and that even then, success is unlikely to last for long . . . or so say our social narratives. Driven by debilitating emotional disturbance, the tortured artist stereotype turns to drugs and drinks to sustain their creative genius. Destitution and death soon cement their fall from grace.

Could society promise creatives a more horrifying destiny? It's no wonder so many writers and artists fail to pursue deeply fulfilling (and, yes, attainable) creative careers. In reality, there has never been a better time for everyday artists to make a living with their creative work. The internet has given today's painters and dancers myriad ways to earn income with their art. The same holds true for countless other creatives, writers included.

Thanks to the internet, self-publishing is easier and more accessible than ever before, as is marketing a book to millions of eager readers. No longer do self-published authors need to stock and ship their books, nor must they hawk their wares at in-person events in the hopes of making a living. With a laptop and an internet connection, nearly anyone can publish and market a book to millions of readers around the globe. And let's not forget that the world's population has never been so big or so literate. Readers abound, writer. Do you see the possibilities?

If you've ever wondered whether it's *really* possible to earn a living as an independent author, then know beyond a doubt that the answer is yes. Building a career as an indie author is entirely possible for countless writers—maybe even yourself. However, I'd be remiss not to mention the role that privilege plays in one's ability to pursue a career as an independent author.

Beyond the time and technological resources needed to write, publish, and market a book, one simply can't produce books that rival one's traditional counterparts without incurring significant expenses. It's also true that very few self-published authors recoup these up-front costs (let alone generate a sufficient income) with the royalties from their debut book. Most indie authors invest years—and several thousand dollars—before they begin earning a full-time living with their writing. The ability to pursue this goal is an undeniable privilege that shouldn't be disregarded as you determine whether self-publishing for profit is right for you.

Moving forward, let's operate under the assumption that you're privileged to have the time, money, and technological resources needed to self-publish for profit. That said, please don't be discouraged if these privileges aren't available to you yet. There are many ways to find joy and fulfillment in your writing life beyond creative employment, and many of the remaining chapters in this book can prove helpful if you're interested in publishing without pursuing it professionally. That said, if indie authorship is a dream you'd like to achieve one day, then take heart. Even if you can't currently pursue this path, you can always take steps to prepare for the journey. For instance, carve out a small, consistent writing routine. Assess your financial situation in search of paths to self-publishing potential. Practice cultivating a positive creative mindset, and make a habit of validating yourself in your creative pursuits. All progress is good progress, writer—and you deserve to live your writing life to the fullest.

Note that I didn't list *talent* among the privileges one needs to publish for profit. As I wrote in *Build Your Best Writing Life*, talent doesn't determine success. It might be a sizable bootstrap with which to pull oneself up, but talent isn't passion. It isn't determination. It isn't damn hard work. Most importantly, *talent* isn't synonymous with *skill*. Yes, you need to be adept at writing, teaching, or storytelling to find success as a self-published author. But nearly anyone with a little passion and determination can acquire these skills. Put in the damn hard work to hone your craft, and talent alone will have nothing on the quality of the work you'll produce.

With this in mind, let's return to the question this chapter endeavors to answer: How do indie authors earn their livings?

Understanding Indie Author Business Models

When preparing to self-publish for the first time, many writers seek a straightforward path to earning a living as an indie author. However, the reality is that indie authors earn their livings in various ways. Some publish multiple books a year, using targeted ads and data-driven campaigns to get their books into the hands of eager readers. Others publish at a slower pace, relying on community-building and networking to grow their readerships and sell more books. Still others use publishing as one leg of their creative empire, cultivating additional income streams through a variety of teaching and speaking opportunities.

In total, there are four main business models indie authors can use as frameworks for developing their creative careers. If you've read *Build Your Best Writing Life*, these business models will be familiar to you. And if you haven't, let's take a moment to discuss each framework for indie author success.

Business Model 1: High-Volume Publishing

With high-volume publishing, authors publish multiple books a year in highly commercial markets to earn a living primarily from royalty income.

The most commercial works of fiction are novels that adhere to strict genre conventions—the type that readers often pop like candy after a long day's work. Think murder mysteries, contemporary romances, and international thrillers. Some high-volume authors use data to identify burgeoning subgenres, penning and publishing multiple books within that niche until the market grows too saturated to quickly make a killing.

This latter type of high-volume publishing can be a lucrative pursuit for some authors, but it's not without risk. Determining whether a tiny subgenre is really on the rise can be a gamble regardless of early data, and repeatedly switching subgenres can complicate the process of developing a dedicated readership. Many high-volume authors find just as much success sticking to tried-and-true genres, even if they have to put in a little more work to make their books stand out from the crowd.

As for nonfiction, the most commercial works are short prescriptive books that guide readers through the process of resolving pain points in their personal or professional lives. Popular genres include finance, spirituality, self-development, hobbies, health, relationships, and technology.

Examples of successful indie authors who follow a high-volume publishing model include Adam Croft (crime thriller),

Christina C. Jones (contemporary romance), Michael J. Sullivan (epic fantasy), Chris Fox (craft of writing and self-publishing), Joseph Alexander (guitar tutorials), and S.J. Scott (self-development/habit-building).

High-volume publishing is the only business model through which authors earn their livings entirely through book sales in the early years of their careers. The remaining three business models will show you how to develop a career as an indie author even if you don't want to publish high-volume.

Business Model 2: Publishing and Teaching

Many indie authors supplement their book sales with teaching opportunities. To find success with this business model, an author typically positions themselves as an authority on a topic and publishes applicable books while supplementing their income with speaking, coaching, or consulting. Others create thriving YouTube channels on their topic of choice or sell relevant digital products such as workbooks, video courses, and online workshops. Alternatively, some indie authors consider themselves teachers first and foremost, choosing to publish books in their field as a way to diversify their income.

Most indie authors who pursue this business model publish nonfiction books. However, it's common for novelists to supplement their fiction income by teaching the writing craft, book marketing techniques, or self-publishing strategies.

Examples of authors who use this business model successfully include Mark Dawson (mystery/thriller, founder of the Self-Publishing Formula), Jenna Moreci (dark fantasy and science fiction, founder of the Writing with Jenna Moreci YouTube channel), and Susan Ariel Rainbow Kennedy, better known as SARK (creativity self-help, founder of Planet SARK).

Business Model 3: Publishing and Patronage

Some less prolific authors turn to patronage to supplement their publishing income, especially in the early years of their careers. For indie authors, patronage typically looks like direct-from-reader support via membership sites like Patreon and Ko-fi. Examples of indie authors who successfully support their careers with patronage include Ksenia Anske (dark fantasy), Tim Pratt (speculative fiction), and Stant Litore (speculative fiction). Jenna Moreci, who was mentioned during the previous section on indie author business models, also supports her work through Patreon. Her platform is a prime example of how these business models aren't mutually exclusive.

Business Model 4: Supported Self-Publishing

One of the most sustainable ways that indie authors develop their careers without turning to high-volume publishing is by maintaining their day jobs. With this business model, an author focuses on building income primarily through book sales rather than supplementing their work with teaching or patronage. However, they rarely publish more than one book a year. Instead, they focus on publishing slowly and sustainably while cultivating dedicated readerships.

Some indie authors pursue this business model with the intention of quitting their day jobs once they can support themselves through book sales alone. Others choose to keep their day jobs while self-publishing as a lucrative, fulfilling side hustle.

This slow-and-steady approach to publishing is perfect for authors who aren't interested in or can't realistically commit to high-volume publishing, teaching, or patronage. This business model is also the most common way writers build their indie author careers—and with good reason. A stable day job is a fantastic investment in your writing career. The steady income allows you to focus on developing your backlist and author platform in the ways you most enjoy rather than do whatever you must to pay the bills. Writing as a side hustle also relieves some of the pressure to succeed that can come with transforming a creative hobby into a career.

The majority of indie authors use this business model in the early days of their publishing journeys. Will you join their ranks?

Understanding Author Platforms

You may have noticed that I mentioned the concept of an author platform while discussing these four business models. An author platform is the foundation from which every author earns their living. Publishing professional Jane Friedman defines an author platform as "the ability to sell books because of who you are or who you can reach." Similarly, I often define this term as an author's capacity for generating revenue as determined by the visibility and credibility of their work.

Unless you're a celebrity, politician, or public speaker, you're unlikely to find commercial success as an author because of who you are. Instead, your capability to reach and engage with readers will determine your success as an indie author. To achieve these goals, most indie authors build platforms that rest upon four cornerstones:

1. A backlist (i.e., the extent of one's published books available for sale)
2. A social media presence
3. An author website
4. An email list

By establishing these platform cornerstones, authors can

engage in various marketing strategies that can help boost their books' reach and revenue. That's why you'll learn how to establish and develop your author platform in part 3 of this book. For now, know that platform-building activities play a key role in helping indie authors earn their livings.

That being said, no measure of striving will help an indie author successfully build their platform and market their work if they don't understand who they're writing for. This knowledge even plays a role before launch day. As you prepare to publish your debut book, you'll take several important marketing steps, including choosing a fitting book title and commissioning an effective cover design. Without a clear understanding of who you're trying to reach, you might fail to make the best pre-publication marketing decisions—and in doing so, you might undermine your book's success long before it hits digital shelves. That's why the next step—identify your ideal reader—is a vital one on your path to indie authorship.

5

THE IMPORTANCE OF DEFINING
YOUR CREATIVE NICHE

I f you'd like to earn income from the books you publish, then you'll need to write with the market in mind. Many writers equate "writing for market" with selling out or creating and publishing only what's most popular at any given time—regardless of one's passion or personal interest—to capitalize on industry trends. This approach to building a career as an indie author is unlikely to be fulfilling. If you aren't passionate about the work you're creating—in other words, if you aren't interested and energized by the subject or story you'd like to write—the challenges of publishing for profit can quickly become soul-sucking trials and tribulations. That said, I don't believe that writing for market and writing for passion are mutually exclusive.

The indie authors who thrive in their careers are those who bring passion and persistence to the table. They understand exactly *who* they're writing for—even if that reader is themselves—and *how* to deliver on that reader's expectations. This is what it means to write for the market: to write with the expectations of your ideal readers in mind.

If you find yourself thinking that you'll never earn a living if you only write for yourself, then take heart. You'll never be the only person interested in reading about the subjects or stories you enjoy. Never before in human history have eager readers had such easy access to millions of titles at their fingertips. And out of all those readers, there is absolutely an audience for the book of your heart. As an indie author, it's your job to identify those readers and get your books into their hands as soon as possible.

To accomplish this, you'll first need a clear understanding of what you write and who you're writing for. I call these two factors your **creative niche**. Taking the time to define your creative niche will help you effectively tailor your work for success at every stage of your writing and publishing journey. With your creative niche in mind, you can revise your books to best meet your ideal readers' expectations. Your creative niche can also help you commission a cover that's likely to attract your ideal readers, write book descriptions and choose listing metadata that increase sales conversions, and craft ad copy and other marketing campaigns that help the right readers know your book exists.

Do you see how powerful a clear understanding of your creative niche can be? To define your niche, take a moment to answer two important questions:

Question 1: What Type of Books Do You Write?

In other words, how would you define the books you write? What genres or categories do they fall into? Which of the following umbrella categories do your books fall?

Literary Fiction

Literary fiction consists of character-driven stories that explore social commentary or the human condition. With a slow pace and an emphasis on nuanced prose, this type of fiction is said to have literary merit (i.e., artistic value). Examples of literary fiction include *The Handmaid's Tale* by Margaret Atwood, *Lincoln in the Bardo* by George Saunders, and *Americanah* by Chimamanda Ngozi Adichie.

Upmarket Fiction

This term often describes literary novels that have commercial appeal. Alternatively, upmarket fiction may describe genre fiction novels with a literary bent. Think complex themes and nuanced prose. This latter type of novel tends to push genre boundaries and may be difficult to categorize as belonging to one particular genre. Examples include *Outlander* by Diana Gabaldon, *Water for Elephants* by Sara Gruen, and *Gone Girl* by Gillian Flynn.

Genre Fiction

Also called commercial fiction, genre fiction consists of fast-paced, entertaining novels that fulfill established genre conventions. In a murder mystery, the killer is always caught. In romance, the lovebirds live happily ever after. Examples of genre fiction novels include *The Notebook* by Nicholas Sparks, *Murder on the Orient Express* by Agatha Christie, and *One of Us is Lying* by Karen M. McManus.

Genre fiction is rife with subgenres that have distinct tropes and conventions. For example, what a reader expects from paranormal romance will vary wildly from what they expect from Regency romance. If you write genre fiction, take the time to familiarize yourself with the subgenres you write in, as meeting readers' expectations is key to your success.

Narrative Nonfiction

As the name suggests, narrative nonfiction consists of books that relay true stories. Memoirs, biographies, true crime books, journalism stories, and travel literature often fall into this category. Some elements of a narrative nonfiction book (e.g., names, dialogue) may be fictionalized to protect anonymity or fill gaps in the author's memory. However, these fictionalized elements should always be indicated in an author's note within the book. Examples include *Untamed* by Glennon Doyle, *The Stranger Beside Me* by Ann Rule, and *A Walk in the Woods* by Bill Bryson.

Expository Nonfiction

Rather than telling a story, expository nonfiction shares information with the reader. Some expository nonfiction books may contain true stories, but these stories are typically quick anecdotes that confirm the author's point rather than the book's primary focus. Expository nonfiction books include everything from self-development and spirituality books to history, popular science, philosophy, parenting books, hobby guides, and more. Popular examples include *A Brief History of Time* by Stephen Hawking, *The Life-Changing Magic of Tidying Up* by Marie Kondo, and *Ego Is the Enemy* by Ryan Holiday.

Poetry

As a form of literature, poetry can be classified as fiction or creative nonfiction. It's also frequently defined by its forms (e.g., sonnets, limericks, haiku) and genres (e.g., epic, narrative, satirical). However, for commercial purposes, contemporary poetry is typically categorized in online marketplaces by its themes, which include the following:

- Love
- Death
- Nature
- Religion
- Spirituality
- Women's issues
- LGBTQIA+ issues

Examples of poetry books include *You'll Come Back to Yourself* by Michaela Angemeer (illustrated by Aleks Popovski), *Clarity & Connection* by Yung Pueblo, and *Sincerely* by F. S. Yousaf.

The Importance of Categorizing Your Books

Some writers, regardless of the nature of their books, recoil from the idea of categorizing or labeling their creative work. Their primary concern is the art. They want to express the story or subject that's weighing on their hearts (or running free and boundless in their minds), and they fear that categorizing their work would make small what they're trying to make big. I understand this fear, but the fact is that books don't sell themselves. If you want to make a profit from your published work, using categories and labels is one of the best ways to help the right readers find your books.

It's OK if your books push boundaries or blend genres. Plenty of readers seek the unexpected. But they'll never get to experience what makes your work unique if you don't give them a way to find your books through online marketplaces. This is where categories and labels come into play. If you're unsure how to categorize your book, consider its primary pull or the aspect of the story that's most likely to draw the attention of readers. Diana Gabaldon's *Outlander* is frequently categorized as historical romance even though it contains time travel and lacks the structure of a classic romance novel. These elements might classify the book as multigenre or even genreless. But at the end of the day, it's the romance between Jamie and Claire that draws readers in and keeps them turning the pages—and that's why the label "historical romance" is best suited to get the book into the hands of its ideal reader.

Question 2: Who Are You Writing For?

The second component of your creative niche is your **ideal reader**, the person who's most likely to love your books. To determine your ideal reader, first consider the demographics that define their identity. Age and gender are two standard demographic markers. Your ideal reader may also be defined by their religion, sexuality, race, nationality, bodily or cognitive ability (i.e., disability, neurodivergence), socioeconomic status, or political views.

You can also distinguish your ideal reader by their unique interests, experiences, or pain points. For example, your ideal reader might love stories that include animals, ice hockey, or turn-of-the-century technology. Alternatively, they may seek books that address their experience with illness or trauma—or more positive experiences like adoption, addiction recovery, or world travel. If you're writing prescriptive nonfiction, your ideal reader will almost certainly be defined by the pain point your books can help them resolve: low self-esteem, unhealthy wellness habits, and procrastination, just to name a few.

Refining Your Creative Niche

Be as specific as possible when defining what you write and who you write for. It might seem counterintuitive to niche down when you're trying to sell *more* books. But if you try to sell your book to everyone, you'll end up selling your book to no one. There are more than seven billion people on the planet, and a good portion of them are avid readers. Even if your ideal reader seems hyperspecific, there's a decent chance that thousands upon thousands of readers would love to get their hands on your books. So give your book its best chance to stand out from the crowd by doing everything in your power to help it appeal to a very specific slice of the market.

This principle is true even if you're writing in a wildly popular genre such as crime thriller or self-development. It doesn't matter whether the type of book you're writing has been done a thousand times before. There's always something that makes your work unique. Maybe it's your voice or writing style. Maybe it's your atypical characters. Maybe it's the themes you address. Whatever the case, lean into that aspect of your creative niche. Indie author Rachel Abbott's debut crime novel, *Only the Innocent*, became a best seller when she centered her first marketing campaign on this tagline: "Women are rarely cold-blooded killers." So be big and loud about what makes your work unique from the countless other books in your genre. That's how you'll find your ideal readers.

Because many authors write books they want to read, their creative niches are likely to reflect their literary interests and identities. For example, some might define their creative niche as any of the following:

- I write Regency romance novels for women who adore headstrong heroines and softhearted dukes.
- I write for Black readers who want to see themselves centered in their favorite epic fantasy adventures.
- I write physical and mental wellness books for older male readers.
- I write beginner cookbooks for new adults who want to learn how to make delicious meals on a budget.

- I write free verse poetry collections that explore the beauty and wonder of my overseas travels.

Some authors prefer to write for a younger version of themselves, which is why their creative niche might look something like the following:

- I write middle-grade adventure novels for children who are struggling with difficult or abusive home lives.
- I write young adult (YA) contemporary novels for hijabi teens who are navigating friendship and romance as they come of age.
- I write picture books that teach early readers about ancient cultures.
- I write personal finance books for teens and new adults who are just getting started in the workforce.
- I write whimsical epic poetry that takes young readers on fantastic adventures.

Some authors write for their children or grandchildren, for readers who share their marginalization or illness, or for those who want to expand their worldview on a particular topic. Other authors simply enjoy writing stories that are primarily read by readers unlike themselves. Consider Nicholas Sparks, who writes romance for a largely female audience, or Robin Hobb, who writes epic fantasy that caters to male readers.

What If You Can't Pin Down Your Creative Niche?

If you're interested in writing multiple genres or for various age markets (e.g., middle grade and adult), your creative niche might be more difficult to define.

If you write vastly different types of books—knitting tutorials and horror novels, for example—then you'll have two ideal readers. To avoid confusion among those readers, it's best to keep your two (or more) types of published works separated. Many authors in similar situations create separate author brands, publishing their books under different pen names and creating separate platforms (i.e., social media presences, websites, email lists) for each type of work. Running multiple author brands can be time-consuming, but ensuring that your books reach the right readers is worth the effort.

However, sometimes there's a common thread that draws readers to most (if not all) of an author's various works. Consider Stephen King's dark story lines or V.E. Schwab's spooky, witchy worlds. As for nonfiction, consider the Chicken Soup for the Soul series, which consists of inspirational story anthologies targeted toward a large variety of readers. If you can identify a similar thread among your demographic-defying work, there's a good chance you have a strong creative niche on your hands.

With a clear understanding of what you write and who you write for, you can now move forward in the self-publishing process with the assurance that you're setting yourself up for indie author success. To ensure that you're stepping into your new identity with a good head on your shoulders, let's quickly discuss the mindset shifts that will help you kick-start your self-publishing journey with confidence and clarity.

6

ADOPTING THE INDIE AUTHOR MINDSET

By now, you've determined your personal definition of publishing success, considered the cost of self-publishing, and concluded that indie authorship is the right path for you. You also understand how indie authors earn their livings, and you're ready to build your career or side hustle as an independent author by developing a platform based on the business model that best aligns with your vision for your creative future. Finally, you've taken a major step toward bringing that vision to life by identifying your creative niche, the unique definition of what you write and who you write for that will guide you in all of your decision-making as a self-published author.

The time has come, writer. You're ready to start your self-publishing journey!

If you're feeling overwhelmed at this point, then know that you're experiencing a perfectly normal response to all the information you've consumed so far, especially if you've never read about or researched the indie author experience before. The wonderful thing about building a career or side hustle as an indie author is that it's a long-term endeavor. You don't need to master every aspect of successful self-publishing overnight.

You have plenty of time to digest and implement what you've learned (and will continue to learn) one baby step at a time.

At this stage, it's also OK if you haven't determined your creative niche, preferred author business model, or definition of publishing success. It's even all right if you're not yet convinced that self-publishing is right for you. Take your time with this experience. Read through the remaining insights and strategies in this book, and chew for a while on what you learn. If you need to experience the self-publishing process before making any decisions about your business model or author platform, go ahead and self-publish a book. There's a reason why we'll discuss the business side of being an indie author in greater detail in part 3—*after* you've learned how to actually prepare and list your book for sale.

As I previously mentioned, this book operates on the assumption that you want to earn income as a published author. If that's not the case, that's OK. There's plenty of information in part 2 that can guide you through the process of producing and publishing your book for personal enjoyment. Feel free to skim what doesn't apply to you to get to the meat of what does. But if you do want to make a living as an indie author, then you might be champing at the bit to get on with the self-publishing process. I applaud your enthusiasm. But if you want to succeed in kick-starting a sustainable career as a self-published author, we have one final foundational factor to discuss.

The Importance of Adopting an Indie Author Mindset

One time, I was chatting with an author I'll call Dylan, who had devoted endless hours to developing his Facebook author page before launching his first book. In the months leading up to publication day, he'd built a following of over 600 readers—which is no small feat for an unpublished author! When publication day arrived at last, Dylan hosted a celebratory launch week on his Facebook page. It should have been a joyous time, right?

When launch week drew to a close, however, Dylan was devastated to learn he'd only sold a few dozen copies of his book. In fact, he was so gutted by this experience that he not only stopped marketing his work—he pulled his book from sale and quit writing altogether. He didn't see the point in sharing his creative work with the world if, in his opinion, all his marketing efforts had amounted to nothing but pennies.

Writer, please don't make the same mistake.

No debut indie author sells hundreds or thousands of copies in the early days of their writing journey. There are no get-rich-quick schemes in the self-publishing world, no overnight successes, and no instant stars. Yes, there are strategies you can use to spike your sales for a limited time. Dylan proved this by selling those few dozen copies of his debut book during launch week—a notable feat given that he'd only been building his platform for a few months without using paid advertising or visibility marketing tactics. The fact, however, is that developing a career as a self-published author is an entrepreneurial act, and it takes time to build a business that turns a significant profit.

To find success as an indie author, you must be willing to think long term. It isn't impossible to make money as an author, but it does take many months—or, more often, many years—of work, especially if you're starting from scratch with no audience or backlist.

It's a shame that Dylan wrongly expected to make it big overnight, because he had the initiative to take charge of his book marketing efforts. This is another mindset you must adopt: the willingness to take an active role in the growth of your indie author business. Too many authors believe that their audience will grow of its own accord if they simply keep writing and publishing books. This is a grievous misconception. Books don't sell themselves, and online book marketplaces won't sell them for you either. As an author, you must be willing to learn, implement, and experiment with the various platform development and book marketing strategies we'll discuss in part 3.

Ultimately, I don't know what contributed to Dylan's lack of persistence. Perhaps there was more to the story than I was told. Nevertheless, an indie author's mindset remains key to achieving financial success. To further strengthen your mindset before embarking on your self-publishing journey, consider adopting the following indie author mental models, which are deeply held beliefs that explain how you view and engage with your creative journey.

Mental Model 1: Commitment Is Key

Indie authors take responsibility for their creative successes, treating their work with the same level of respect and professionalism as one would in any other career. They forge strong work habits and make a point of consistently showing up to work. Like any professional, they take occasional sick days and vacations. However, they don't allow moods, motivation deficits, or distractions to keep them from writing. They recognize that motivation is most often the *result* of action rather than the *cause*, and they employ strong work habits to cultivate momentum in their creative careers. They live by a popular quote that's attributed sometimes to William Faulkner and other times to W. Somerset Maugham: "I only write when inspiration strikes. Fortunately, it strikes every morning at nine o'clock sharp."

To implement this mental model, consider building a tiny writing habit. Determine when you'll write (e.g., every weekday before work), and choose a small goal to complete each session (e.g., "I will work on my novel for ten focused minutes"). Resist the urge to go big or go home, especially in the early days of your new writing habit. Small goals make new habits easier to adopt, and the habit you sustain will always take you further than the habit you don't sustain.

Mental Model 2: Failure Is a Launchpad

Successful indie authors recognize that at various points in their publishing journeys, they'll experience what others may perceive as failures. They'll write books that will struggle to rise through the sales rankings. They'll receive many one-star reviews. They'll try marketing strategies that don't boost their book sales and spend money on tools and services that fail to live up to the hype. But successful indie authors don't view these incidents as failures. Instead, they treat them as valuable learning experiences, actively gleaning lessons and insights they can harness to redirect their efforts for the better.

Adopting this mental model can be difficult. It's easy to react negatively to perceived failures. The trick isn't to banish every negative thought or emotion that crops up. Instead, you must view perceived failures with mindfulness. The next time you feel like you've fallen short, ask yourself why. Sometimes perceived failures are entirely out of your control. You can't help if a reader leaves a negative review on a book just because it wasn't their cup of tea, for example. However, when asking yourself why reveals a misstep or missed opportunity, then a small dose of mindfulness should reveal the action steps you can take to do better next time.

Mental Model 3: Doubt Is a Springboard

As I first discussed in *Build Your Best Writing Life*, successful authors don't treat doubt as an obstacle to overcome or a weakness to suppress. Instead, they recognize doubt as an indicator of a potential issue that often presents itself in the form of a question (e.g., "Am I not good enough to write this story?"). Rather than internalizing this issue as a limiting belief (e.g., "I'm not good enough to write this story"), successful indie authors coolly consider the issue at hand. They dig to the root cause of the issue and take necessary steps to resolve it (e.g., "My plot isn't working because I'm not familiar enough with story structure yet," or "I'm going to do some research"). This mindful approach helps indie authors harness doubt as a springboard for creative growth.

To implement this mental model, continue cultivating a practice of mindfulness in the face of negative thoughts and feelings. The next time you feel inadequate in your creative work, ask yourself why. What potential issue is rumbling through your mind? After you identify this issue, work proactively to resolve it. Sometimes doubt is nothing more than a fear you need to brave. Other times, doubt raises a genuine issue that requires action to resolve. In the latter case, do the research. Ask for feedback. Take the break you need to rest and recover. Do whatever you need to do to find the solution to your issue and, ultimately, harness doubt as a springboard for growth in your creative journey.

Mental Model 4: Fortune Favors the Enterprising

Successful indie authors recognize that the industry rarely stagnates. They understand that the platform development and book marketing strategies they currently employ might prove less effective over time, so they take proactive action to ensure their continued success. They study industry trends and changes, explore new marketing efforts, and learn the ins and outs of new technologies that might impact their creative work.

Implementing this mental model is easy. By picking up this book, you've already taken the initiative to expand your book

marketing knowledge. Make a point of consistently consuming applicable books, articles, podcasts, and videos, and you'll have no trouble adapting to changes in the indie author experience.

Mental Model 5: The Journey Is the Reward

There will always be more books to write, more money to make, and more room to grow one's readership. For this reason, successful indie authors don't view their goals as destinations they must reach to find joy and fulfillment in their writing lives. Instead, they reject their egos and utilize their goals as guideposts, reveling in everyday challenges and accomplishments as they enjoy every step in their publishing journey.

If you tend to stake your creative fulfillment in big-picture achievements rather than everyday joy, this mental model might seem out of reach. As someone who's been in that situation before, I know the feeling. But this doesn't have to be the case. To enjoy every step in your creative journey, make a point of cultivating pride in your everyday efforts. For example, after each writing session, take a moment to complete this prompt: "I'm so proud of myself for . . ." Be your own cheerleader. Pump yourself up. Validate your creative work, no matter how big or small the achievement. It's hard to lack joy in your writing life when you're actively identifying the reasons to be proud of your skills, projects, and commitment to your craft.

Preparing to Self-Publish

So what do you say, writer? Are you ready to adopt the indie author mindset and embark on your journey to self-publishing success? If so, then put on your climbing shoes and prepare to tackle the learning curve. In part 2, we'll explore how you can produce and distribute high-quality books that hold the power to attract and maintain the attention of your readers.

PART II

PRODUCING AND PUBLISHING YOUR BOOK

PART II

PRODUCING AND PUBLISHING YOUR BOOK

7

REVISING YOUR MANUSCRIPT FOR PUBLICATION

Your ability to iron out your manuscript's issues, errors, and inconsistencies is limited by your subjectivity. You're simply too familiar with your manuscript to make it the best it can be on your own. This is why collaborating with freelance editors and other people who can provide feedback is an essential part of the pre-publication process. Another set of eyes can catch mistakes you wouldn't catch on your own, and another reader can make suggestions that will strengthen your manuscript in ways you might never have considered before.

In chapter 3, we defined and discussed the four types of freelance editing an author may seek as they polish their manuscripts: developmental editing, line editing, copyediting, and proofreading. Some writers also seek professional feedback from **sensitivity readers** who specialize in critiquing the portrayal of sensitive topics (e.g., the representation of a marginalized character, a traumatic event) from their own lived experience.

We'll talk more about how to hire freelance editors and sensitivity readers (including what to expect from the process and how to set yourself up for a positive experience) later in this chapter. But first, let's discuss what may be the most popular type of external feedback sought by indie authors: beta readers.

Working with Beta Readers

Beta readers are everyday readers who provide authors with casual feedback on their unpublished manuscripts, helping them identify key story issues and other developmental concerns. Because beta readers aren't professionals and typically provide feedback for free, authors on tight publishing budgets may choose to seek beta feedback instead of paying for developmental editing. Others might employ beta feedback after completing an early draft of their novel to ensure that their story is on the right track.

Established authors often source beta readers from their email lists, but don't worry if you haven't established your author platform yet. Many writers find their beta readers via the online writing and reading communities on social media. Consider getting involved in at least one platform (preferably where your ideal readers hang out) as soon as possible. If you have no idea where to begin, check out Mixtus Media, where social media marketing expert Jenn Hanson-dePaula teaches authors how to develop their readerships and market their work on social media.

Many authors prefer to work with beta readers who read widely within their genre. After all, a devoted romance reader probably wouldn't offer the best feedback on a horror novel. Many indie authors also prefer to source beta feedback from other writers, since writers tend to have the necessary craft knowledge to provide the most constructive criticism.

Because they're unfamiliar with your manuscript, beta readers can critique your work with greater objectivity than you can. Still, they're only human, so their perspectives will always be colored by their personal preferences and experiences. One reader's opinion doesn't necessarily indicate a major story issue or needed change. This is why most writers seek feedback from multiple beta readers at once, using patterns in the feedback they receive to direct how they revise their work.

It's common for an author to work with anywhere between five and twenty beta readers at a time. Some even seek feedback from what can only be described as a small army of beta readers. I became an unwitting general myself when sourcing beta feedback for *Build Your Best Writing Life*. After putting out the call for feedback and receiving far more interest than I'd expected, I found myself giving marching orders to twenty-seven beta readers. In the end, rounding up so many willing soldiers proved a wise strategy given that some readers resigned before providing feedback while others performed poorly in the field, so to speak. (In other words, their feedback was too kind or shallow to be helpful.) When in doubt, adding a few extra beta readers to the mix is the way to go.

Understandably, it can be nerve-racking to send your unpublished work out for critique. As you prepare to send your manuscript to beta readers, you might find yourself fiddling with comma placements, rewriting perfectly acceptable sentences, or even doubting the quality of your work altogether. We'll talk more about how to handle constructive criticism with grace later in this chapter. But for now, know that you don't need to polish your manuscript to a high shine before sending it out for feedback. Any beta reader worth their salt will understand that they're reading a draft rather than a finished book, and they'll critique your work accordingly. On the flip side, do respect your readers' time and effort by ensuring that your story is readable. A little light editing can make all the difference.

As for how you'll send your manuscript to beta readers,

most are A-OK with reading your book in PDF format or as a Microsoft Word document. If you're feeling fancy, you may want to offer your draft as an EPUB file for e-readers as well, which you can easily compile using most modern word processors (e.g., Microsoft Word, Scrivener, Google Docs). If your manuscript is on the longer side, many beta readers will likely find an EPUB file a welcome courtesy, since reading long documents in other formats can be tiresome.

To ensure a positive beta reading experience for everyone involved, communication is key. Be clear about the type of feedback you'd like to receive and when you'd like to receive it—and be sure to take the length of your project into account when setting a deadline. No one's going to read and review a 75,000-word novel in just a few days. Several weeks is more realistic.

To encourage the most helpful feedback, many authors provide beta readers with an optional list of questions they can answer, such as the following:

Example Beta Reader Questions
Fiction or Narrative Nonfiction

- Did this story hold your attention? Where did you lose interest?
- Did you find any scenes boring, confusing, or difficult to follow?
- Was the plot well paced? Did it flow logically?
- Did the characters feel real to you? Did you understand their motivations?
- Did you get a clear idea of the setting in each scene? Did you find the setting descriptions immersive?
- Did the dialogue feel authentic for each character?

- Was the ending satisfying? Were there any loose ends that I need to wrap up?
- Is there any other feedback you'd like to add?

Example Beta Reader Questions
Expository Nonfiction

- What did you like about this book? What parts did you find most interesting or helpful?
- Were any parts of the book not as interesting or helpful?
- Were any chapters or concepts confusing or unclear?
- Did it feel like anything was missing from the book? Would you like to see any sections expanded? If so, which ones and why?
- Did the book have a logical flow? Do any chapters or parts need to be rearranged?
- Were you bored at any point in the book?
- Did the book have a clear mission and audience?
- Did the book leave you feeling inspired and empowered? Did you find the content actionable?
- Is there any other feedback you'd like to add?

Working with Freelance Editors and Sensitivity Readers

After defining common self-publishing expenses and your publishing budget during chapter 3, you should have an idea of the types of professional feedback you'd like to seek. Which should you employ first? Given that there's little point in restructuring sentences before revising content (in other words, tackling the small stuff before the big stuff), you should always seek freelance editing in the following order:

- Developmental editing or technical feedback
- Line editing
- Copyediting
- Proofreading

Bear in mind that editors and sensitivity readers are often booked several months in advance, so it's best to search for your first editor as soon as you can estimate when your manuscript will be ready to send their way. After nailing down an editing timeline with your first editor, you can then query the next to book a spot in their schedule. Just be sure to give yourself a few extra weeks in between editing partnerships to make any necessary changes to your manuscript and to account for any last-minute scheduling adjustments.

Not sure where to find potential editors? Check out my list of recommended editors in *The Ultimate Self-Publishing Toolkit*, a free PDF download available at https://www.well-storied.com/toolkit. As for sensitivity readers, you can find helpful databases at https://www.writingdiversely.com/directory and https://sensitivityreaders.tumblr.com.

As you research potential editors, know that not every editor will be the right fit for you and your book. Some editors might not work in your genre. Others might not have availability in their schedules that works with your timetable or offer services at a rate that fits your budget. Still others might not be well trained or as professional in their work as they claim to be.

Whenever possible, query editors who are well known or have been personally recommended to you by another author. Many editors offer testimonials from past clients on their websites. If any of those testimonials come from an author with a public email address (i.e., one you can find on their author's website), then don't hesitate to ask the author if they'd be willing to share more details about their experience working with their editor. Remember that editing can be expensive. It never hurts to do your research before biting the bullet and paying the bill.

Querying editors about their services and availability doesn't have to be a scary process. Many editors offer detailed contact forms on their websites to make querying as simple as possible. If an editor doesn't provide such a form, you can reach out via email using the Editor Query Template in the textbox below.

Editor Query Template

Hi, [EDITOR'S FIRST NAME],

My name is [YOUR FULL NAME]. I'm looking for a [TYPE OF EDITOR] for my [TYPE OF NOVEL]. After reviewing your website, I think you would be a great fit for this project.

[TITLE OF PROJECT] is a [SHORT BLURB]. The manuscript is approximately [WORD COUNT] and has been [LIST ANY PRIOR FREELANCE EDITING OR FEEDBACK]. [INSERT PREFERRED START DATE OR DEADLINE FOR EDIT IF YOU HAVE ONE].

If you're interested in this project and have availability in your schedule, I'd love to discuss a potential collaboration and receive a quote for your services. I've attached a sample from my project to this email for your consideration. If you need any further information, please don't hesitate to ask.

Thank you for your time and consideration!

Best wishes,

[YOUR FIRST NAME]

———

However, before querying an editor, be sure to review their website to ensure that you aren't asking them for information they've already provided publicly.

Did you notice that in the Editor Query Template, I mentioned attaching a sample of your project? Many editors are willing to complete a **sample edit** (i.e., a free edit on a small portion of your manuscript) to help you determine whether they're a good fit for your project. Before attaching an excerpt from your manuscript to your query, be sure to review the editor's website for any sample edit procedures. An editor may indicate how long the excerpt should be, how it should be formatted, or which part of the manuscript the excerpt should come from. And if an editor's website doesn't explicitly mention sample edits, don't be afraid to ask for one. For example, you could add the following to your query email: "If you're interested in taking on this project, I would love to receive a sample edit of your work. Please let me know your preferred procedures." Most editors are happy to complete a sample edit, as doing so helps them determine whether a project is one they'd like to take on in return.

Rates, Quotes, Contracts, and Payments

Editors often structure their rates per hour, per page, or per 1,000 words. The type of rate you receive may differ depending on the type of editing you're seeking.

While most editors list standard rates on their websites, always request a firm quote for your project before signing any contracts. If an editor devises their rates per hour of work, they may request a sample edit before offering a quote to gauge the number of hours they'll need to complete the requested work. For example, Sarah Kolb-Williams lowered her standard copy-editing and proofreading rates for *Build Your Best Writing Life* after she reviewed my sample edit, which I suspect was in such good shape thanks to the tireless work of my brilliant line editor, Sara Letourneau.

For this reason, it may be worth querying an editor even if their listed rates are slightly outside your budget. While an editor is unlikely to slash their standard rate or quote in half, many are willing to negotiate to a small degree. If the quote you're given is higher than you expected, you can use the Rate Negotiation Email Template below to see if they're willing to negotiate.

Rate Negotiation Email Template

Hi, [EDITOR'S FIRST NAME],

Thank you for providing a quote for [TYPE OF EDITING] for my project, [TITLE OF PROJECT].

Based on your sample edit, I know your editing style is a great fit for this project. Unfortunately, the quote you provided is a bit outside my budget at this time.

I respect the work you do and understand if your rates are firm. However, if you're open to negotiation, I'd love to discuss how we could reach a rate that works for both of us. Thank you again for your time and consideration.

I look forward to hearing from you!

Best wishes,

[YOUR FIRST NAME]

Once you and your editor have agreed on a quote and a timeline for the project, your editor should provide you with a formal contract that outlines project expectations (e.g., deadlines, installment due dates, scope of work). If your editor doesn't offer a contract, request one before making any payments, as a contract will provide legal protections for both you and your editor.

After you receive a contract, read it carefully before signing it, and don't be afraid to raise any questions or concerns with your editor. Ensuring that terms are agreeable for both parties is key to a successful partnership. Also, be sure to save a copy of the digital contract. While you're unlikely to need this document down the road (especially if you've done your due diligence and hired a reputable editor), it's always better to be safe than sorry.

One of the expectations listed in your contract should be payment due dates. Editors typically charge for their services in installments, which not only makes editing expenses less intimidating but also helps hold both parties accountable to the terms of the contract. For instance, authors won't receive their edits until they've issued at least one down payment, and editors won't be paid in full until they've completed the contracted work.

Feel free to negotiate with your editor if a greater number of installments would make the cost of commissioning their services less of a burden. Also, most editors use third-party apps like PayPal or QuickBooks to issue invoices, which you can pay using your preferred payment option (e.g., credit card, debit card, bank transfer).

Understanding the Editing Process

Depending on the type of editing you've commissioned, you may receive your editor's feedback in one (or more) of several forms. Large-scale developmental feedback is often provided in the form of an **editorial letter**, a multipage write-up that breaks down your editor's constructive criticism. Most editors also work within the manuscript itself, leaving feedback through comment boxes or making in-line edits with Microsoft Word's Track Changes feature. (Don't worry—these changes aren't permanent unless you want them to be.) After receiving the edited manuscript, you can review all of your editor's tracked changes, accepting or rejecting each one as you see fit.

While most editors work in Microsoft Word, don't worry if you don't have this program. Most word processors allow you to export a file as a DOC or DOCX file that you can send to your editor, while the tracked changes your editor makes in Microsoft Word can be reviewed using the free Google Docs app. Unfortunately, Google Docs runs slowly when loading a large, heavily edited file. If you don't already have Microsoft Word, you may find it worthwhile to purchase a one-month subscription any time you need to review an editor's notes or changes. Alternatively, many public libraries offer access to computers that have Microsoft Word installed.

After reading through your editor's feedback, don't be afraid to contact them with any questions you have. Editors want to help you create the best version of your manuscript, and they can't help you fulfill this mission if you don't understand their comments or changes. Knowing this, many editors offer to schedule a video call to address your concerns directly. Others may opt to answer your questions via email or as comments in the manuscript itself. If you'd prefer one option or the other, be sure to let them know up front.

Finally, if you're on a tight budget, you may want to invest in

freelance editing over other services. Many free book formatting options exist, and you can always upgrade your cover
design post-publication. However, you can't undo public negative reviews that critique your book's sloppy content or writing.
Invest in the quality of your manuscript first and foremost, and
you'll save yourself a world of time, money, and heartache later
in your publishing journey.

Handling Constructive Criticism with Grace

Whether you've recently received feedback from a beta reader,
editor, or technical reader, resist the urge to immediately open
the email and dive right in. Constructive criticism can be difficult to process. It's never a bad idea to ensure that you're in the
best possible headspace before reading all the suggested
changes you may need to make to your beloved manuscript.

When you do crack open the feedback you've received,
remember that good criticism is *constructive*. It exists to help
make your book the best that it can be, not to tear you down or
tell you that you're a terrible writer. If someone does criticize
your manuscript in a genuinely destructive way, don't hesitate
to dismiss their words. Their criticism says a lot more about
them than it does about you and your work.

That said, it's a good idea to assume positive intent when
reviewing constructive criticism. Most editors and beta readers
don't intend to hurt your feelings. Rather, they want to help you
and your work succeed. If a comment does sting, take a
moment to ask yourself why. More often than not, the note only
hurts because of that fragile ego we talked about in chapter 2.
We all have our insecurities, and feedback that triggers these
insecurities can be difficult to process. Still, there's no need to
spiral into doom and despair should the bite of criticism come
snapping at your heels. Instead, remind yourself that perceived

failures are opportunities for growth. When criticism offers you a challenge, seize it.

On a less emotional note, always apply feedback mindfully. You don't have to make every suggested change or accept every tiny edit. Remember, you get to decide what stays and what goes. So try to adopt a more objective mindset, and be honest with yourself about what's truly best for your story. But always go with your gut in the end. It's your book, after all. If you aren't happy with the end product, then what's the point?

Finally, remember to show your gratitude to those who help you polish your manuscript for publication. It takes a village to raise a book. Your editors and beta readers won't see their names listed front and center on your book's cover, but their work is still invaluable. Consider showing your appreciation by sending them a thank-you card or email, listing their name(s) in your book's acknowledgments, or sending them a signed and personalized copy when your book is published.

8

FINALIZING YOUR BOOK'S CORE METADATA

After finalizing the content of your manuscript, the next two steps in the book production process are to format your manuscript for publication and commission (or purchase) a cover design. However, you can't complete these steps without first finalizing your book's core metadata: your author name, the book's title, and the book's description.

These three pieces of **metadata** (i.e., secondary data that provides information about a primary piece of data) are integral to your book's ability to generate reach and revenue. In fact, it's common for indie authors to periodically update details for books that aren't selling as effectively. For example, Joanna Penn—a *USA Today* best-selling indie author whose creative business brings in multiple six figures each year—originally published her fiction and nonfiction books under her given name. Then, several years into her publishing journey, she realized the importance of separating her brands to avoid reader confusion and republished her international thrillers under the pseudonym J. F. Penn. Similarly, she retitled several of her novels when they received negative reviews from Christian readers who were disappointed to discover the books' secular content. *Pentecost* became *Stone of Fire*, *Prophecy* became *Crypt of Bone*, and *Exodus* became *Ark of Blood*—all more effective titles for secular books that feature religious motifs.

Do you see how this metadata can make or break the success of your publishing experience? If you previously self-published a book that you're now interested in updating, you'll benefit from reading the "Updating and Relaunching Older Books" section of chapter 20 in addition to this chapter. Unfortunately, changing a book's author name, title, or description can be costly and confusing for readers. That's why it's important to carefully consider your book's core metadata from the start. So let's explore best practices for choosing an author name and book title and writing a description for your book.

Selecting an Author Name

An **author name** is a real or fictional name under which an author publishes their book. It's the same name that appears on the cover of a book. But an author name doesn't have to be your real name. There are many reasons why an author may choose to publish under a **pseudonym** (i.e., a fictional name, a pen name) instead. For example, an author may want to use a pseudonym for any of these reasons:

- Maintain their privacy
- Separate their creative work from a primary career
- Publish under a more memorable name
- Publish under a name that better fits the tone of their genre
- Distinguish their work from another author or public figure with a similar name
- Publish various types of books under individual pen names to separate author brands and avoid reader confusion

- Avoid using a given name they dislike

Regardless, modern circumstances don't necessitate the use of a pseudonym as heavily as history once did. Women no longer need to assume male pen names to find financial success in the publishing industry, just as authors with non-Western names are finding increasing success in Western markets. The normalization of a wide range of topics and stories also means that fewer writers need to use pseudonyms to avoid scandal. Nevertheless, pen names still have their place in the modern publishing landscape.

If you'd like to publish under a fictional author name and you intend to earn income as an indie author, then it's important to bear the concept of branding in mind. Readers are more likely to purchase books from authors they know and trust—which means, by extension, that name recognition sells. Therefore, choose a pseudonym that's distinctive, memorable, and befitting of your creative work.

When considering a pseudonym, ask yourself the following questions:

- **Does your chosen name flow when read aloud?**
  The easier your name rolls off the tongues of your readers, the more likely they are to remember it.
- **Is your chosen name relatively easy to spell and pronounce?** Readers will have trouble remembering and searching for your author name if it's both unusual and complicated to spell.
- **Does the tone of your chosen name match the genre you're writing in?** Judith Rumelt likely had an easier time reaching YA fantasy readers by publishing under the pen name Cassandra Clare.
- **Is your chosen name believable?** Unless you're writing a parody, readers will likely find on-the-nose

names like Ogre Bloodaxe or Hope Lovejoy off-
putting.
- **Can you imagine answering to your chosen name?**
  If you don't like the idea of readers calling you by
  your pseudonym, it might not be the right choice for
  your work.

Ultimately, the choice is up to you. If you're comfortable
using your given name and feel it's a good fit for your work, go
ahead and use it. But if you're interested in publishing under a
pen name, then consider options that distinguish your work
and befit your creative niche.

Choosing a Book Title

Your book's title is a high-value marketing tool because it
impacts the first impression readers will have of your book.
Ensuring that your title attracts and intrigues your ideal
readers is key to effective book marketing.

When brainstorming book titles, keep your creative niche
in mind. A good title works in tandem with cover design to
relay the book's genre, tone, and intended audience. If you
aren't sure where to begin, consider perusing popular
published books in your general niche, and make note of titles
that strike your interest.

As you complete this market research, you may discover a
formula for titles that are trending in your niche. For example,
"[NOUN A] of [NOUN B] and [NOUN C]" was a popular title
trend among YA fantasy novels in the 2010s. Consider *A Court of
Thorns and Roses* by Sarah J. Maas, *Daughter of Smoke and Bone*
by Laini Taylor, and *Children of Blood and Bone* by Tomi
Adeyemi, among others. That same era saw an influx of
contemporary romance titles that featured the protagonist's full
name. *Evie Drake Starts Over* by Linda Holmes, *The Two Lives of*

Lydia Bird by Josie Silver, and *Get a Life, Chloe Brown* by Talia Hibbert are all popular examples. If you stumble upon a trend in your niche and plan to publish your book within the next few months, you may want to capitalize on the trend by giving your book a similar title. Alternatively, you may want to avoid trendy formulas in favor of titles that feel more timeless within your genre. The choice is up to you.

In any case, don't make the mistake of choosing a title solely because it blends in with those of comparable books in your niche. Effective book titles don't just relay genre and audience. They also tie directly in with your book's core content, hinting at important story details and themes or striking at the heart of the problem your book works to solve. For more detailed guidance, consider these titling tips for the following various types of creative work.

Novels

While there's no exact science to choosing a fantastic book title, patterns do emerge when we take a broader look at the titles of popular novels. For example, character-driven stories (i.e., stories that feature internal or interrelational conflict) tend to have titles that address the story's themes or contain the protagonist's name, nickname, or identifying title. Consider examples such as the following:

- *Outlander* by Diana Gabaldon
- *Atonement* by Ian McEwan
- *Me Before You* by Jojo Moyes
- *The Fault in Our Stars* by John Green
- *The Book Thief* by Markus Zusak
- *The Lovely Bones* by Alice Sebold
- *Finnikin of the Rock* by Melina Marchetta

- *Life of Pi* by Yann Martel

Alternatively, plot-driven stories (i.e., stories that feature external conflict) often have titles that focus on an unusual setting, an object of importance, or a momentous event. Plot-driven book titles may also feature a group of protagonists or a notable secondary character who helps drive the plot. Take some of the following titles, for instance:

- *Six of Crows* by Leigh Bardugo
- *The Lightning Thief* by Rick Riordan
- *Jurassic Park* by Michael Crichton
- *The Reptile Room* by Lemony Snicket
- *The Golden Compass* by Philip Pullman
- *The Da Vinci Code* by Dan Brown
- *The Hunger Games* by Suzanne Collins
- *The Eyre Affair* by Jasper Fforde

Some popular titles will prove to be effective exceptions to these patterns. Consider Colm Toíbín's award-winning literary novel *Brooklyn*, which is named for its setting rather than its protagonist or theme. Set during the age of immigration, the story's backdrop symbolizes growth and change, which are two themes that the novel explores in depth.

Alternatively, rather than breaking the mold, many book titles combine elements from the patterns mentioned above. Consider *The Girl Who Loved Tom Gordon* by Stephen King, *The Lord of the Rings* by J. R. R. Tolkien, and *Harry Potter and the Sorcerer's Stone* by J. K. Rowling.

Expository Nonfiction

The most popular forms of expository nonfiction are prescriptive nonfiction (i.e., how-to books that seek to solve a problem in the reader's life) and educational books that teach readers about topics of interest. In either case, the titles of popular books in this genre tend to follow one of two conventions. First are straightforward titles that cut right to the core problem or topic a book discusses. This type of title can be especially effective because it utilizes keywords that readers may search when trying to find a particular type of book. Consider titles such as these:

- *Astrophysics for People in a Hurry* by Neil deGrasse Tyson
- *How to Make a Living as a Writer* by James Scott Bell
- *Set Boundaries, Find Peace: A Guide to Reclaiming Yourself* by Nedra Glover Tawwab
- *Seasonal Slow Knitting: Thoughtful Projects for a Handmade Year* by Hannah Thiessen

The title of the book you're reading, *Self-Publishing Simplified*, also falls into this convention.

Alternatively, you may want to consider giving your expository nonfiction book a flashy or sensational title that catches the eyes of your ideal readers. Take the following titles, for example:

- *Let's Get Digital: How to Self-Publish, and Why You Should* by David Gaughran
- *Eat That Frog! Get More of the Important Things Done Today* by Brian Tracy
- *The Power of Now: A Guide to Spiritual Enlightenment* by Eckhart Tolle
- *You Never Forget Your First: A Biography of George Washington* by Alexis Coe

Be sure to clarify the core problem or topic your book discusses with a subtitle that uses appropriate keywords.

Narrative Nonfiction and Poetry Collections

If you're writing a memoir, travelogue, or book of personal essays, the heart of your book likely lies in the themes it explores. The same often holds true for poetry. That's why pivotal themes often appear in the titles of narrative nonfiction books and poetry collections. Consider the following examples:

- *Hunger: A Memoir of (My) Body* by Roxane Gay
- *Not My Father's Son: A Memoir* by Alan Cumming
- *Untamed* by Glennon Doyle
- *The Sun Will Rise and So Will We* by Jennae Cecelia
- *Home Body* by Rupi Kaur
- *Call Us What We Carry: Poems* by Amanda Gorman

While these patterns (and exceptions) may help you brainstorm ideas for your book's title, know that they aren't a strict rule of thumb. If you brainstorm a fantastic title for your book that doesn't match any of these conventions, don't kick it to the curb. As long as it works in tandem with your book's cover design to entice your ideal readers, it's a great option.

Crafting a Book Description

Your book's title and cover design may work together to attract your ideal readers, but your book's description is what will convince them to buy the book. Sometimes conflated with **back cover copy** (i.e., the descriptive copy that appears on the back of a book's print editions), a **book description** is the sales text that appears on your book's online sales pages. The nature of a good book description depends on its genre and intended audience, but its primary purpose is to convince readers that your book will be their next great read. Many authors dread the process of writing a book description. It's not easy to pitch a book in just two or three enticing, largely spoiler-free paragraphs. However, the process doesn't have to be as painstaking as you might expect. The best way to simplify the description-writing process is to study the descriptions of popular comparable books. If you write contemporary romance, research current best-selling contemporary romance books on Amazon. Study each book description to get a feel for the language, structure, and cadence of how great descriptions in your genre are written. Also, consider these tips for crafting descriptions for various types of creative work.

Novels

Effective fiction descriptions dress up the book's premise, the punchy statement that distills the heart of a story into two or three sentences. If you haven't crafted the premise for your book yet, here are the key story elements it must contain:

- The protagonist(s)
- The setup (i.e., the catalyst that kick-starts the story's plot)
- The protagonist's goal or desire
- The antagonist or the source of emotional resistance
- The core conflict
- The protagonist's essential relationships (when applicable)
- The protagonist's motivation (if possible)

Note that a premise isn't an outline. It doesn't need to include a story's resolution, identify characters by name, or detail any major plot points. It simply needs to provide an overview of a story's core narrative arc. Need an example? Consider this premise I wrote for Talia Hibbert's best-selling romance novel *Get a Life, Chloe Brown*:

> After a near-death experience {motivation}, a chronically ill website designer {protagonist} decides to stop hiding from life by creating a bucket list she plans to complete as soon as possible {goal or desire}. First up? Move out of the comfort of her family's mansion and into her very first apartment {set-up}. But when romance sparks between the timid computer geek and the gruff but handsome apartment superintendent {essential relationship}, she must decide whether she's truly brave enough {source of resistance} to take a chance on love {core conflict}.

Defining your story's premise will clarify the core narrative elements that should appear in your book description. In fact, writing a great book description is often as simple as adding an emotional hook and specific details (i.e., character names, places) to your premise, then rewriting the prose to be as interesting and genre-specific as possible. Most fiction descriptions then end with a literal or figurative question that hooks readers' interest. Search *Get a Life, Chloe Brown* online to see how its description follows this formula.

Expository Nonfiction

Readers usually pick up expository nonfiction books because they're looking for information on a specific topic. Therefore, the description for this type of book should immediately hook readers with a sentence that highlights the core problem or question that the book will resolve.

After the hook, the description should expound on the problem or question at hand, driving home readers' need for the book. It should then outline the key ways in which the book will resolve readers' questions or curiosity. To distinguish its major points, expository nonfiction descriptions often include diverse formatting. Think bullet points, headings, and bolded or italicized text. Pertinent keywords and relevant expertise (e.g., a degree, awards, professional titles) can also improve the effectiveness of your description.

Finally, in *How to Market a Book*, Joanna Penn recommends that nonfiction authors employ the age-old copywriting trick of inserting readers into the book description through the use of *you*. She advises authors to avoid telling readers what they'll teach in the book in favor of sharing what readers will learn. You can see this concept in action by reviewing *Self-Publishing Simplified's* book description.

Narrative Nonfiction and Poetry Collections

As with any book, the descriptions for narrative nonfiction books and poetry collections should start with a hook. This hook should strike at the emotional core of the book; in many cases, it may be a direct quote from the book itself. Consider this hook from Roxane Gay's memoir *Hunger*: "I ate and ate and ate in the hopes that if I made myself big, my body would be safe."

Descriptions for memoirs and personal essay collections often use the following formula. After delivering an emotionally resonant hook, the description uses third-person language to introduce readers to the author and explore how the book's primary themes became relevant in the author's life. The description then outlines how the author will explore these themes throughout their book.

Descriptions for poetry collections often follow a similar formula, highlighting the primary themes that the poems explore. For example, Mary Oliver's *Devotions* collects the most timeless and impactful poems from her decades-long career. The title alludes to Oliver's lifelong devotion to poetry and the natural world, as well as to the reverent tone Oliver often used in her writing. To reflect this, the description for *Devotions* explores both her career and her commitment to honoring nature through her art.

Perfecting Your Book Description

No matter what type of book you're writing, remember that a good description is short and enticing. It ditches lyrical prose and detailed data for simple, powerful language that tells readers why the book will be their next great read. And don't forget to copyedit or proofread your book's description. Some readers might not notice or care about spelling mistakes or misplaced commas. However, most will assume that the state of a book's description is indicative of the state of its content—and no one wants to read a book riddled with poor writing and numerous errors. So give your book description the respect it deserves as a powerful book marketing tool, and you'll ensure that your ideal readers can't wait to get their hands on a copy.

9

FORMATTING YOUR BOOK FOR PUBLICATION

Good writing may play a major role in keeping readers engaged in a book, but don't underestimate the power of quality formatting. If you've ever struggled to parse text that features a heavily stylized font, poor line spacing, or nonexistent margins, you already understand how design can make or break a book's readability. Of all the reasons a reader might fail to finish your book (or worse, leave a negative rating or review online), unprofessional formatting is one you can easily avoid. So how do you properly format a book for publication?

Since formatting can be a tedious process, many authors choose to commission an interior book designer to complete this task for them. Book design companies like Damonza, Mibl-Art, and Ebook Launch offer formatting packages, some of which charge less than $100 for e-book formatting. You can also connect with freelance interior book designers through online freelance marketplaces such as Upwork, Fiverr, or Reedsy. The latter is an online marketplace specifically designed to connect authors with editors, book formatters, and other freelancers involved in book production and marketing.

One thing to bear in mind when commissioning professional formatting is that each edition of your book (e.g., paperback, e-book, large print) must be formatted separately. The more editions you publish, the greater your formatting expenses will be. And should you need to request any updates (e.g., fixing typos or other small errors) to your book's interior design post-publication, you can expect an additional charge per format.

On a positive note, most freelance book formatters and book design companies offer great discounts on bundled book formatting services (e.g., e-book and paperback). So keep an eye out for great deals if you intend to outsource this work. You can find a list of recommended book design companies and freelance interior book designers by downloading my free self-publishing tool kit at https://www.well-storied.com/toolkit.

To produce a high-quality self-published book, consider working with skilled and experienced professionals—such as editors and cover designers—whenever your budget allows. However, book formatting is the one pre-publication task that most authors can complete on their own without risking an amateur result. This is thanks to the various easy and effective DIY formatting options available on the market. While formatting your book requires time and effort, most DIY formatting options are free or far more cost-effective than commissioning book formatting services. DIY options also make it easier (and cheaper) to update your book's text post-publication.

With that in mind, let's explore the five most common options indie authors choose for formatting their books. Note that all prices are listed in US dollars.

Option 1: Vellum

Vellum is a book formatting app with an intuitive interface and easy design options that make formatting a manuscript for print and e-book distribution a cinch. It offers great design options for fiction and nonfiction books alike and requires very little know-how before use. Formatting a book with Vellum is as simple as uploading your manuscript, assuring the text within each chapter is assigned the proper text styles (e.g., a heading is formatted as a heading), and choosing from a variety of designs to determine how you'd like each text style to appear.

In addition to formatting a manuscript, you can use Vellum to compile advance review copies (ARCs), add clickable store links to your e-books, and assemble box sets. These features, combined with the ease of using the app, make Vellum a favorite book formatting option for many indie authors. I've used Vellum to format all of my published books, including *Self-Publishing Simplified*, and I have no intention to switch to a different option moving forward.

Unfortunately, Vellum is only available for Mac users at this time. However, many authors have reported success in using the app on a PC using the work-around method outlined by indie author Paul Teague on his website https://www. paulteague.net.

Out of all the DIY book formatting options discussed in this chapter, Vellum requires the biggest up-front investment. The app's e-book license is priced at $199.99, while the license for print and e-book formatting costs $249.99. On the bright side, you only need to purchase a Vellum license when you're ready to export a finished file for publication. This means you can trial Vellum for as long as you'd like before committing, even going so far as formatting multiple editions of your book in full. And because you only need to purchase a license once, Vellum becomes more cost-effective with each book you publish. For example, I've used Vellum to format six editions of two books, and it has cost me just $41.67 to format each edition I've published (or $125 per book). With more books on my publishing agenda, it won't be long before formatting a book with Vellum will cost me pennies on the dollar.

Overall, Vellum is a great DIY formatting option for authors who plan to publish multiple books as well as those who are looking for the easiest, most intuitive way to DIY their books' formatting. For extra guidance, you can find a free Vellum video and text tutorial on my website at https://www.well-storied.com/vellum.

Option 2: Scrivener Compile

If you're a Scrivener user, you have an easy formatting option at your fingertips. This word processing app, which is popular among writers for its many features that simplify the process of developing long-form content, includes a book formatting tool called Compile. It allows you to, well, *compile* your manuscript into various formats, including popular **trim sizes** (i.e., the dimensions of a printed book) and e-book editions.

To format your book with Scrivener, you will follow nearly the same process as you would when working in Vellum. First, you assign each document within your project a section type (e.g., heading, section). Next, you assign a particular design style called a layout to each section type to alter its appearance. The number of design styles available within the Scrivener Compile tool is limited, making it a less elegant option than other DIY formatting tools. But if you're already a Scrivener user and looking to create a simple, highly readable interior book design for free, the Scrivener Compile tool is an excellent option.

Option 3: Book Design Templates

Across the internet, you can find a variety of easy book design templates that are compatible with popular programs such as Apple Pages, Microsoft Word, and Adobe InDesign. Some of the most popular templates were created by the late Joel Friedlander, who was an industry-leading book designer, and are sold online through his company, Book Design Templates. Its website offers a variety of templates for books of all genres, literary styles, and age markets. These templates can be used to format both print and e-book editions of a book at the same time and are compatible with the three popular programs mentioned above. They're also fully customizable, so you can tweak any and every feature to your liking.

The templates at Book Design Templates are available for a single-book license of $59 or a multibook license of $79, making this interior design option perfect for authors looking for easy and affordable DIY formatting.

Alternatively, if you're on a tighter budget, you may enjoy formatting your book with one of author Derek Murphy's five interior design templates that are compatible with Microsoft Word and Adobe InDesign. These templates are available for free download via Murphy's website https://www.diybookformats.com. Just bear in mind that you'll still need to purchase Microsoft Word or Adobe InDesign if you don't already use either program.

Option 4: Microsoft Word

If you're a Microsoft Word user with decent formatting knowledge (or the willingness to learn), you don't need a book design template to format print and e-book editions of your book.

Various online tutorials—many of which are available for free on YouTube—walk you through the process step by step. Formatting with Microsoft Word is a more tedious and time-consuming process than other DIY book formatting options. However, it's a great choice for current users who don't mind putting in the time and effort to use this largely free formatting option.

Option 5: Adobe InDesign

If you're savvy about graphic design, DIY-minded, and eager to produce a detailed book design that can rival the more elegant books produced by big-name publishers, Adobe InDesign should be your weapon of choice. While this formatting option isn't for the faint of heart, it's an affordable choice for those with the technical and design knowledge needed to produce a phenomenal interior book design. As with Microsoft Word, you can find numerous Adobe InDesign book formatting tutorials for free on YouTube.

Understanding Book Trim Sizes

Any writer can format their manuscript without much book design knowledge. Easy formatting options like Vellum, Scrivener's Compile tool, and the majority of book design templates do all of the hard work for you; you only need to decide on basic design styles before your interior book files are ready for publishing. But no matter which formatting option you choose, there's one piece of book formatting you'll need to understand: trim sizes.

Whether you're commissioning an interior book design or doing it yourself, you can't have your book formatted for print if you don't know what size you want your printed book to be. These dimensions—the length and width of your printed book

—denote your book's trim size. Common paperback trim sizes in the United States include the following:

- 5½ × 8½ inches (paperback)
- 5 × 8 inches (paperback, large-print paperback, hardcover)
- 6 × 9 inches (paperback, large-print paperback, hardcover)

Common international paperback trim sizes include the following:

- 198 × 129 millimeters (paperback)
- 216 × 135 millimeters (paperback, large-print paperback, hardcover)
- 234 × 156 millimeters (paperback, large-print paperback, hardcover)

To choose the best trim size for your book, measure a few books within your genre and your desired edition. You may also want to do some online research to find out whether certain trim sizes are more common in your genre. If your manuscript is on the shorter side (e.g., less than 60,000 words), you may want to choose one of the smaller standard trim sizes (e.g., 5½ × 8½ inches, 198 × 135 millimeters) to ensure that your printed book doesn't appear too thin. And if your manuscript is on the larger side, you may want to choose a larger standard book size instead.

Generally speaking, however, any of the trim sizes listed above will be an excellent fit for a professionally produced, full-length book—and with that decision made, you'll have a formatted interior book file ready for publication in no time.

10

COMMISSIONING A COVER DESIGN

Despite the saying, readers *do* judge books by their covers —and rightfully so.

Most readers discover new books by perusing online marketplaces. When scrolling through a list of books in their genre of choice, they're looking for covers that catch their eye. Covers that make them stop and consider whether that book might be their next great read. To convert that interest into clicks, your book's cover design and title must work in tandem to denote your book's genre, tone, and intended audience. If you package your paranormal romance in a sparkly pink cover with a generic title like *First Kiss*, you probably won't catch the attention of those looking for their next steamy tale of vampire–werewolf love. Moreover, the readers who purchase your book based on its title and cover alone will probably be in for quite the shock. Oops! But trade the sparkles for a dark, shadowy cover and a title like *First Bite*, and you're back in business.

With that in mind, let's discuss how you can procure a cover design that will attract your ideal readers and ultimately help you sell more books. All prices are listed in US dollars.

A Quick-Start Guide to Cover Design

First things first: Now is *not* the time to DIY. Unless you have experience with graphic design and a strong understanding of professional book cover standards, any cover you create is unlikely to be as attractive and commercially effective as its traditionally published counterparts. Fortunately, high-quality book cover design doesn't have to break the bank. While you'll need to commission an individual cover for each edition you plan to publish (e.g., e-book, paperback, large print), many freelance cover designers and book design companies offer premade e-book covers for less than $100.

Premade covers are more affordable than custom cover designs because they aren't created with a particular story in mind. Instead, they feature generic but genre-specific designs that authors can buy for exclusive use at any time. Within a few days of purchasing a premade cover, the designer will add your title, subtitle, and author name to the design, then send the finished files your way. Some designers may make small changes to the design (e.g., font or color changes) at your request, though they may charge an additional fee for this work. Most premade covers are treated as a single product and won't be resold, which means you'll have a one-of-a-kind cover design that costs a fraction of the price of a commissioned cover.

That said, there's no doubt that commissioning a custom cover design is the surest way to procure a cover that will effectively attract your ideal readers. With that in mind, let's break down everything you need to know to commission a cover that's unique to your book.

Working with a Freelance Designer or a Book Design Company

If you'd like a custom cover for your book, you can commission a design from a freelance cover designer or a book design company. Both options are valid, but there are a few differences between them that you'll want to consider.

First, freelance cover designers typically offer specialized services, creating covers exclusively for books that fall into the handful of genres they specialize in. They also tend to work more closely with authors through video calls or extensive design briefs (more on this in a moment) to ensure that they create the best possible design for each book. Because their work is highly specialized, freelance cover designers often have slower turnaround times than book design companies (e.g., two to four weeks once they begin work on the project). A freelance designer may not be a good fit for your project if you need a cover sooner rather than later.

How much does it cost to work with a freelance cover designer? This will depend on several factors, including the freelancer's rates, the difficulty of the work required to create the best design for your book, and the number of editions for which you'd like to commission a cover. That said, it's common for freelance cover designers to charge $500 or more for an e-book cover design—a price that reflects the many hours they'll spend creating a highly specialized, professional cover for your book. If you plan to produce at least one paperback edition of your book, expect to pay over $1,000 for your bundled cover designs.

Some freelance cover designers post base rates for their services on their websites, but you'll likely need to submit a **design brief** to receive an exact quote for the type of cover(s) you'd like to commission. This brief also helps designers determine whether your project is a good fit for their schedules and expertise.

Alternatively, you may want to consider commissioning a cover from a book design company such as Damonza, MiblArt, or Ebook Launch, among other options that are popular among seasoned indie authors. Typically, book design companies are willing to create covers for books of any genre, and their rates are often standardized and posted on their websites with order forms that make commissioning a custom cover design a cinch. These rates tend to be more affordable than those proposed by freelance cover designers because the work isn't as specialized and the process is less collaborative. Many custom e-book covers from design companies start at $299 or less, with combined e-book and paperback cover packages starting at $399.

As I mentioned earlier, most book design companies have a faster turnaround time than freelance cover designers, and they can often prepare an initial draft of the custom cover design in just a few business days. This, combined with their more affordable rates, makes a book design company a great option for authors looking for quality midrange covers that will help the right readers find their books.

Understanding Design Briefs

Regardless of whether you work with a freelance cover designer or book design company, you'll most likely need to submit a design brief to initiate the custom cover design process. A design brief is a document that lists the information a designer needs to create a great custom cover for your book. This information includes the following:

- Your book's title and subtitle
- Your author name

- What your book is about
- A description of your ideal reader
- Design elements you'd like to see on the finished cover (e.g., characters, colors, objects)
- The cover editions you'd like to commission (e.g., e-book, paperback, audiobook)
- The deadline by which you'd like to receive your cover

When commissioning a cover design for a print book, you'll also need to note the trim size you've chosen and the length of the formatted manuscript, as both factors directly impact the dimensions of your cover design. Be sure to review chapter 9 if you've yet to format your book for publication.

Writing a design brief doesn't have to be difficult or overwhelming. In fact, most cover design companies provide easy prompts as part of their checkout process, while freelance cover designers often offer guidelines on their websites that you can use when getting in touch with them. After submitting your brief, you and your designer will have a conversation via email, phone call, or video chat to ensure that they understand what you're looking for in your cover design (or to offer ideas, if you have no idea what kind of cover you'd like to commission). This conversation will help your designer revise your brief and determine an official quote and timeline for the cover design project when applicable.

Throughout this process, remember that communication is key. If you want to receive a cover you love, be up front and honest with your designer about whether you're happy with the direction your design brief is heading. While most designers are willing to revise their initial designs to a degree, it's always best to avoid a total cover design overhaul by being clear about your expectations before work on your design begins.

Cover Design Contracts and Payments

If you commission a custom cover design from a design company, you'll likely sign a contract (or check a box stating that you agree to specific terms and conditions) during checkout. If you're working with a freelance designer, you'll receive a contract *after* you and the designer have agreed on the design brief you've developed for the project. Either way, a cover design contract exists to set project expectations in stone and hold each party legally accountable to their end of the agreed-on terms. As always, be sure to read this contract in full, and don't hesitate to bring any concerns to your designer's attention before signing.

Among other details, a cover design contract should list your finalized quote and the terms for paying for the service. Some companies and designers charge for their services up front, but many will split the quote into two installments: one you'll pay before work begins, and one you'll pay when you're happy with the finished design. As with editing services, don't be afraid to have a conversation with your designer if you'd benefit from paying in more installments.

Requesting Revisions and Finalizing Your Cover Design

Once the stated turnaround time has passed, you'll receive the first draft of your custom book cover design via email. With any luck, you'll love the cover your designer has created. However, know that it's OK to request revisions if you're not a fan of a particular aspect of the design, such as the choice of font or the color of a small motif. Revisions are a normal part of the design process, and your contract should include at least one round of minor changes free of charge.

Don't despair if the cover design you receive fails to meet the mark on a larger scale, though. A few options are available to you should this happen. If your designer somehow misunderstood the design brief you discussed with them, they should be willing to design a new draft that meets your expectations. Alternatively, if they've created a design that technically fits your brief but doesn't tickle your fancy, you can likely commission a second design at a discounted rate.

However, if worst comes to worst and you receive a design that fails to meet the quality you expected, you have the right to back out of the contract and take your business elsewhere. In my experience, a reputable cover designer or book design company will respect your wishes and refund any payments you've already made. If the designer or company is unwilling to refund your initial payment, you may be able to recoup that expense using the protections provided by the online payment company (e.g., PayPal, Stripe) that processed your transaction. Regardless, you'll likely have a great experience when you commission a custom book cover.

Once you're happy with the design you've received, let your designer know and they'll send the finalized files your way. Expect to receive a JPEG file for the e-book and audiobook covers and a PDF for print covers, which you'll later upload when creating your book's listings—a process we'll explore in the next three chapters.

11

UNDERSTANDING DISTRIBUTORS AND AGGREGATORS

I n the traditional publishing industry, an author's publisher coordinates the printing and distribution of their book. Authors who publish independently don't have this advantage. Instead, they prepare and upload their book for print and digital distribution through online book distribution companies such as Amazon's Kindle Direct Press (Amazon KDP). This responsibility may seem overwhelming at first, but the process of publishing your book with an online distributor is quite simple. All an author needs to do is create a listing via their distributor(s) of choice as follows:

1. Upload their finalized cover and interior book files.
2. Fill out their book's listing information (e.g., categories, book description, metadata).
3. Click the Publish button.

Most distributors will then review your submission manually. As long as your book files and metadata meet the distributor's requirements, your listing will be approved and available for sale within seventy-two hours—and often in twenty-four hours or less. Awesome, right?

Some distributors exclusively publish digital books (i.e., e-books). Others, like Amazon KDP, Barnes & Noble Press, and IngramSpark, also offer print-on-demand (POD) services through which they'll print and ship physical copies of your book directly to the readers who order them. This means you'll never have to stock and ship books yourself unless you'd like to sell signed, personalized copies through your website or at an in-person event. Many distributors also allow you to make your books available for sale to schools, libraries, and physical book-stores around the world.

Most distributors allow authors to upload their books for free, then pay authors through a royalty agreement similar to those that traditionally published authors sign when inking their book deals. However, as previously discussed, indie authors often earn much higher royalty rates than traditionally published authors, since they're producing the books them-selves. Most distributors offer authors between 60 and 80 percent per sale, with 70 percent being the most common royalty rate. That being said, some distributors slash royalty rates for books priced below average (e.g., $0.99), since these books have a smaller profit margin. Again, please note that all prices in this chapter are listed in US dollars.

With all of this established, you may be wondering which distributors you should use to list your book for sale. Before you make this decision, there's a far more important question you'll need to answer.

Will You Go Wide or Stay Exclusive?

As the world's leading book distribution platform, Amazon KDP offers authors various financial incentives to publish their e-books exclusively with Amazon.

Through a program called KDP Select, an author can submit one or more of their e-books to be included in Kindle Unlimited (KU), an Amazon subscription service that gives readers access to thousands of books for a set monthly fee. Inclusion in this program allows authors to earn a share of the KDP Select Global Fund, the monthly pool of cash from which KDP Select authors are paid based on a per-page-read rate called the Kindle Edition Normalized Page Count.

In layman's terms, enrolling an e-book in KDP Select means that you can share your e-book with readers who use KU and then earn income based on how many pages of your book are read per month. Taking part in KDP Select also gives you access to exclusive book promotion tools such as Kindle Countdown Deals, through which you can run a limited-time discount on your e-book through Amazon.com and Amazon.co.uk and earn a bonus 70 percent royalty rate on sales made to customers in Mexico, Japan, India, and Brazil.

The only catch to these great opportunities? By enrolling an e-book in KDP Select, you sign away the right to sell that e-book anywhere else online (including through your website) for ninety days. When that period is up, you can opt out of KDP Select, manually re-enroll in the program for another ninety days, or set up auto re-enrollment.

If you continually enroll an e-book in KDP Select, you're choosing a publication path that indie authors often call "staying exclusive." The alternative—"going wide"—refers to opting out of KDP Select in favor of retaining the right to list an e-book through multiple distribution platforms. But which option is right for you?

Because sales made through Amazon comprise the bulk of the income for most indie authors, staying exclusive can be an attractive option. KU users tend to be avid readers who consume multiple books per month, and many purchase books outside the program after discovering authors they love. With this in mind, KDP Select can be a gold mine for authors who write longer novels (e.g., epic fantasy, science fiction) or publish easy-to-devour book series. However, staying exclusive with KDP Select as a long-term strategy can be risky, since Amazon retains the right to change its payment structure and exclusive benefits at any time—and they have in the past, with some authors reporting a significant drop in sales revenue afterward.

Because staying exclusive leaves one largely beholden to Amazon's authority, some indie authors don't view exclusivity as a truly independent publishing option. The alternative is going wide, listing your book for sale through multiple distribution channels to reduce the risk of sudden financial loss. Going wide enables authors to reach a wider pool of potential readers, including those who don't have access to an Amazon marketplace or who take issue with the company's controversial business practices. Cultivating a broader range of income streams also provides authors with greater long-term financial stability and success. However, going wide does come at the cost of the income and exposure you could earn by opting in to KDP Select.

If you'd like to write full-time, going wide to diversify your income and expand your global reach is likely the right choice for you, especially if you're concerned with minimizing your long-term financial risk. On the flip side, if you have a book or series that would be a great fit for KDP Select and you'd like to earn as much as possible ASAP, enrolling in KDP Select could be a great option as long as you understand the risks.

Some authors have reported finding it easier to cultivate income in non-Amazon markets when they have multiple books to sell. For this reason, these authors seek to maximize their income at all stages in their publishing journey by staying exclusive with Amazon KDP until they have multiple books to sell via wider distribution channels.

Ultimately, there's no right or wrong answer to the question of exclusivity. The choice is up to you, and only you can know what's best for you and your books. Regardless of whether you go wide or stay exclusive with your e-books, you'll need to determine the platforms you'll use to distribute the print editions of your books. With that in mind, let's look at the platforms that indie authors use most often to list their books for sale.

Exploring Common Book Distributors and Aggregators

When publishing a book, there are two types of platforms you can use to create a listing: distributors and aggregators.

Distributors—also known as direct distribution platforms —allow you to list your book for sale in the specific marketplace(s) each platform serves. Creating a listing with Amazon KDP, for example, ensures that your book will be available for purchase through Amazon's worldwide marketplaces. Other popular distributors include Barnes & Noble Press, Apple Books, Google Play, and Kobo Writing Life. Listing your book for sale with multiple distributors can be time-consuming, since authors must create (and, in many cases, update) a listing for each platform. However, using a direct distribution platform also ensures that you'll earn the highest possible royalty rate on book sales.

If all of this work sounds exhausting, you're in luck. **Aggregators** such as IngramSpark, Draft2Digital, and Smashwords simplify the process of going wide by allowing you to create a single listing that they'll distribute to multiple marketplaces of your choosing. Aggregators also make it possible for you to access dozens of online markets that lack direct distribution platforms, including numerous library apps, book subscription services, and global online bookstores. The only downside is that aggregators tend to charge an up-front listing fee or a 10 percent fee on sales to account for their extended reach. For that reason, many authors (myself included) prefer to upload directly to the most popular direct distribution platforms, then use an aggregator(s) to maximize the reach of their books.

NOTE: There are a few popular aggregators I chose not to include in this chapter because of their exploitative fee structures. If I haven't mentioned them, there's a good chance I don't recommend them.

Working with Print-on-Demand Distributors

If you plan to publish your book in at least one printed format (e.g., paperback, hardcover, large print), you'll need to create a listing with a POD distributor.

As I mentioned earlier, POD distributors print and ship books on your behalf each time you make a sale, which means you never have to stock and ship books yourself. Before the launch of the world's first e-reader in 2007, POD services first made full-time indie authorship accessible to nearly any writer with internet access. These services can still be used today to offer physical books to the wide array of readers who prefer holding a physical copy in their hands over pressing an On button.

The most popular POD distributor is Amazon KDP, which you can use to list and sell paperback copies of your book in worldwide Amazon marketplaces. You can also select Amazon KDP's Expanded Distribution program to make your paperback available to libraries, bookstores, and academic institutions.

If you'd like to go wide with the print editions of your book, you can use Barnes & Noble Press to sell paperback editions of your book in Barnes & Noble's online bookstore. You can also use aggregators like IngramSpark and Draft2Digital to offer paperbacks through dozens of extended marketplaces.

Offering a hardcover edition of your book is trickier. Most

POD platforms don't support hardcover printing because of its high print production cost. The resulting profit margin is simply too small to make hardcover printing worthwhile for the distributor—and, in most cases, for indie authors. While creating a hardcover edition of your book may be an exciting prospect, the reality is that most indie authors who produce hardcovers never see a return on their investment. Even if the cost of commissioning a cover design and interior book file for a hardcover edition isn't too steep, industry sales figures reveal that the vast majority of readers simply don't purchase hardcover books, probably because of their expensive list prices.

Regardless, if producing a hardcover is important to you, you aren't completely out of luck. Through Amazon KDP and IngramSpark, you can create and distribute a hardcover edition of your book to multiple marketplaces. Other POD distributors also offer this service, but do your research before committing. As I mentioned earlier, if I didn't name a particular distributor or aggregator in this chapter, there's a good chance I don't recommend them because of their exploitative fee structures. There's simply no reason to pay hundreds of dollars to list your book in global marketplaces you can otherwise access for $49 or less.

Some writers worry about the quality of POD paperbacks. Unfortunately, it's common for errors to occur during printing, leading to reader complaints about poor-quality paperbacks. However, these types of errors occur across the board within the publishing industry. My local library once stocked an unreadable copy of *Dune* by Frank Herbert—a traditionally published book—for years before purchasing a replacement. To reduce the risk of readers receiving poorly bound or misprinted books, avoid exploitative POD distributors who are more likely to work with low-quality printers. And should any misprinted copies slip through the cracks, readers are always welcome to request a new copy from the distributor free of charge.

As mentioned, POD enables authors to sell physical books without having to stock and ship them out of their own houses. But what if you'd like to order multiple physical copies to sign and sell at an in-person event or through your author website? Good news: all major POD distributors allow you to order multiple copies of your book at print or wholesale costs. But let's not get too far ahead of ourselves. You can't revel in the experience of signing books for adoring fans without first uploading your book for sale. That's why I'll walk you through the process of creating your first listing with an online distributor in the next chapter.

12

LISTING YOUR BOOK FOR SALE

B y now, you've decided whether you'd like to go wide or stay exclusive, and you've determined which distributors you'd like to work with. With those decisions made—and with your finalized book cover and interior files in hand—it's time to upload your book for sale by creating your first listing. But what if you're not ready to publish your book just yet? No worries! With most distributors, you can save a listing as a draft so that you can work on the listing at your own pace or prepare your listing ahead of your intended publication date.

While the process of creating a listing is unique to each distributor, most platforms prompt you to enter similar information about your book. With that in mind, let's review the most common types of information you'll input when crafting your book's listings. Unless otherwise noted, all prices are listed in US dollars.

NOTE: This chapter will include a few special notes concerning Amazon KDP, which features the most complex listing process.

Type 1: Primary Metadata

Your book's primary metadata includes information such as its title, optional subtitle, and language, as well as your author name. If you're publishing under a pen name, that's the name you'll want to enter for this prompt.

Type 2: Your Book's Description

Also known as a blurb or back cover copy, your book's description is the information readers can view on the listing page to learn more about your book. If you've already written back cover copy as part of the print cover design process, enter that information in this section of your listing. If you haven't written a description yet, refer to the tips and guidance provided in chapter 8 to craft your book's blurb.

In addition, you may want to note your book's **content warnings** (i.e., cautionary statements about events or language within your story that some readers might find triggering). You can also use this space to clarify the nature of your story (e.g., sweet versus steamy romance). However, be wary of including information that's often forbidden under platforms' terms of use, such as book reviews, testimonials, review requests, and keyword lists, as well as discount notices and any content that's widely considered offensive or obscene.

Type 3: Contributors

Most distributors and aggregators will ask you to list the names and roles of any creatives who contributed to your book's content, such as a cowriter or an illustrator. Refrain from listing editors, beta readers, and critique partners in this space. "Contributors" refers exclusively to professional collaborators who helped cocreate (rather than revise and polish) your book.

Sometimes "editor" is included in a drop-down menu listing contributor roles. In this case, "editor" refers to a person who has compiled an anthology. For example, George R. R. Martin and Gardner Dozois edited *Rogues*, a short story anthology. If you aren't publishing an anthology, avoid adding an editor as a contributor to your book in this section. Instead, credit the freelance editors who helped shape and polish your manuscript in your book's acknowledgments.

Type 4: Edition Number

If you anticipate making significant changes to your book's content down the road (e.g., to update data based on new research), you can list your book's edition number. Otherwise, you can leave this prompt blank if you don't anticipate making major changes.

Type 5: Keywords

Keywords are single words or short phrases that readers are likely to enter when searching for your book in online marketplaces. Keywords help marketplace algorithms determine where, when, and to whom they should show your book, so choose your keywords wisely.

Take care to avoid words and phrases that are included in your book's title, subtitle, and description, as well as in your categories. The algorithm already pulls information from these elements, so entering these words and phrases as keywords would be redundant. Instead, consider entering some of the following effective types of keywords:

- Settings (e.g., Regency-era England, small-town America)
- Themes (e.g., coming-of-age, forgiveness)

- Tone (e.g., feel-good, grimdark)
- Character roles (e.g., single dad, female detective)
- Tropes (e.g., enemies to lovers, found family)

Alternatively, if you're writing expository nonfiction, consider these effective keyword types:

- Pain points (e.g., back pain, consumer debt, low self-esteem)
- Core topics (e.g., orchestras, professional basketball, world travel)
- Reader aspirations (e.g., toned arms, spiritual wellness, organized home)
- Ideal reader (e.g., recent college graduates, aspiring actors, home cooks)
- Writing style (e.g., academic, humorous, persuasive)

If you'd like to maximize your book's visibility, an advanced tool like Publisher Rocket can help you research your book's most applicable and competitive keywords.

Type 6: Categories

A category is a subsection of books in an online marketplace that share key characteristics. Think of categories as sections in a bookstore. Stores tend to feature each section's best-selling books, including them in displays, placing them on endcaps, and stocking them with their covers facing out. This increased visibility helps the book continue to sell well. To receive similar visibility online, choose niche categories in which your book can thrive. For example, you'll have a much easier time climbing sales rankings—and reaching your ideal readers—in a niche category like "Gaslamp Fantasy" than in a broader category like "Teen and Young Adult Fantasy."

Most distributors and aggregators offer a wide variety of categories for listing your book. However, none can top the internet's leading book distributor, Amazon KDP. With over 16,000 categories to choose from, you shouldn't have too much trouble finding niche choices that are a great fit for your book. An easy way to discover niche categories is to research the listings of published books within your genre. On Amazon, you can find a book's categories in the "Product Details" section of its listing.

However, you might find that Amazon doesn't offer its full range of categories as options you can choose when creating your book's listing. This is because Amazon has already begun categorizing your book using the metadata you've entered. Don't let this keep you from getting your book into the niche categories where it's most likely to thrive, though. Instead, tell the Amazon algorithm how *you* want it to categorize your book by strategically including your desired niche categories in your book's keywords and description. You can also contact Amazon KDP's support team to request that your book be included in a particular category.

You can find a full list of Amazon's available e-book and paperback categories by searching for the "Browse Categories" article in the Amazon KDP Help Center. You can also learn more about how to maximize your book's visibility with categories by reading the free article titled "Secret Method to Choosing the Best Amazon Categories" by Dave Chesson at https://kindlepreneur.com/how-to-choose-the-best-kindle-ebook-kdp-category.

Type 7: Miscellaneous Metadata

Many distributors and aggregators will prompt you to enter optional miscellaneous metadata about your book, such as a reader age range, preorder information, and whether your book contains adult content. Some may prompt you to indicate whether your book is a large-print edition, while others may ask whether you'd like to enable digital rights management (DRM). We'll talk more about the latter in a moment.

Type 8: Print Settings

If you're creating a listing for the print edition of your book, you'll need to select ink and paper types. Most authors use black ink to save on print costs (and thus increase profit). However, there's a disparity between paper types. Often, authors and publishers print expository nonfiction books on white paper for a crisp learning experience. On the flip side, many novels, narrative nonfiction books, and poetry collections are printed on cream paper for a warmer reading experience. Ultimately, the choice is up to you.

When defining print settings, you'll also need to note your book's trim size and finish type for the cover. You already determined the trim size in chapter 9, before commissioning a cover design and formatting your book for print. As for cover types, you can choose between a matte finish or a glossy finish. A book's finish is rarely determined by its content. Instead, it's a matter of design preference on the author's or publisher's part. If you're unsure which option you'd prefer, you can purchase proof copies of each finish so that you can review both of them in person. Finally, you'll need to indicate whether your book contains **bleed** (i.e., content printed at the edge of a page, such as an illustration). Note that all of the above factors may impact printing costs.

Should You Enable DRM?

When creating an e-book listing with some distributors, you'll need to determine whether you'd like to enable **digital rights** management (DRM), a digital "lock" intended to prevent unauthorized digital sharing and book piracy. This may sound great at first, and you're welcome to enable DRM if you'd like. However, I recommend *against* doing so for one reason: enabling DRM does more to punish honest readers than it does to deter pirates.

In reality, DRM is an incredibly easy lock for digital pirates to pick. If someone wants to pirate your DRM-enabled book, a quick Google search can tell them how to do so in a matter of minutes. However, for everyday readers, DRM-enabled e-books are almost impossible to access on more than one device. This means that if a reader purchases a DRM-enabled e-book through Amazon, they can only read that e-book on a Kindle e-reader or in the Kindle app. If they ever want to switch to a different brand of e-reader or reading app, they'll lose access to their entire digital library of DRM-enabled books. For obvious reasons, this lack of accessibility is a huge hassle—one that has led a subsection of readers to avoid buying DRM-enabled books entirely. Ouch.

Understanding ISBNs and Imprints

As I mentioned during chapter 3, an **ISBN** is a thirteen-digit code that serves as a book's unique identifier. Libraries, online distributors, and bookstores use ISBNs to track book sales and stock purchases.

Most online distributors don't require ISBNs for e-books. However, authors must purchase ISBNs to assign to every other edition of their book, including paperbacks, hardcovers, and audiobooks. The only exception to this rule lies with Amazon KDP, which offers authors free ISBNs they can assign to any print editions of their books. However, it's important to understand that ISBNs are issued in a publisher's name. This name is then made public alongside other metadata that readers may find on your book's listing page.

If you choose to use Amazon KDP's free ISBN for print books, Amazon will publicly register your ISBN as being published by "independently published." While there's nothing wrong with this, many full-time indie authors prefer to present their books more professionally by creating their own publishing trade name, or their own version of an imprint. The authors can then use their imprint to purchase ISBNs to assign to their books. For example, if you were to view the listing for *The Snowdonia Killings* by indie crime author Simon McCleave, you'd see that the book was published under the imprint Stamford Publishing. Similarly, Christina C. Jones's best-selling self-published romances are listed under her Warm Hues Creative imprint.

If you'd like to add this professional touch to your self-published work, know that creating an imprint isn't as difficult as it seems. To establish an imprint, simply register a new business with your local government under your publishing trade name of choice—a step you'll likely want to take for tax purposes, in any case. You can then use that name to purchase ISBNs through the official ISBN issuer in your home territory.

If you plan to go wide with the print edition of your book, you'll need to purchase ISBNs regardless of whether you register your imprint as a proper business, as most distributors don't provide ISBNs free of charge. Unfortunately, ISBNs can be pricy. Just one ISBN purchased through Bowker, the official ISBN agency for the United States and Australia, costs $125. On the bright side, ISBNs are much more cost-effective when purchased in bulk. For example, Bowker offers a set of ten ISBNs for $295 or a set of 100 ISBNs for $575.

While this expense may seem a steep price to pay for a thirteen-digit code, it's important to remember that ISBNs allow you to publish widely. Armed with ISBNs, you can cultivate a broad range of income streams through dozens of online retailers, physical bookstores, and libraries. With a little patience and persistence, the cost of purchasing ISBNs can pale in comparison to the revenue you'll earn from the income streams they enable.

Confirming Your Creative Rights

At some point in the listing process, you may be asked to confirm that you hold your book's copyright and publication rights. These rights are inherent to your work the second you put words on the page, and you retain these rights until the moment you sell them to a second party. As long as you haven't inked a book deal with a traditional publisher—and as long as you wrote the book yourself or with a co-writer who consents to publication—you're good to go.

Pricing Your Book for Sale

To price your book, you may need to indicate whether you hold the rights to publish your book worldwide or only in certain territories. If you wrote your book yourself and haven't sold any publishing rights, you can publish your book in all territories. But if you're creating a listing through Amazon KDP, you'll need to select your primary Amazon marketplace. This isn't necessarily your home marketplace, but rather the marketplace in which you expect to sell the most books. For example, an author in the United Kingdom may list their primary marketplace as Amazon.com rather than Amazon.co.uk if they expect to sell their books primarily to US-based readers.

If you're listing an e-book through Amazon KDP, your next step is to choose your royalty plan: 35 or 70 percent. You can choose the 70 percent royalty plan if your book meets the following requirements:

- You plan to list your e-book for at least $2.99 but no more than $9.99.
- Your e-book list price is at least 20 percent less than the list price for the print edition of the same book on Amazon.
- You make the title available for sale in all possible territories.

If your book doesn't meet these requirements, you'll need to choose the 35 percent option. And if you're publishing a print book, you'll earn a standard 60 percent royalty rate minus print costs, a formula that reads as follows:

$$(\text{royalty rate} \times \text{list price}) - \text{printing costs} = \text{royalty}$$

For example, if you choose to list your print book for $9.99, and your book costs $3.55 to print, you'll earn $2.44 per sale because of the following:

$$(0.6 \times 9.99) - 3.55 = 2.44$$

After selecting your preferred royalty plan where applicable, it's time to set your book's list price. To choose the best list price for your book, consider the following:

- How similar books in your chosen categories are priced
- How much you'd like to earn per sale
- E-book delivery costs or print costs

Let's say you'd like to earn $2.00 on every e-book you sell. Amazon charges $0.15 per megabyte to deliver your e-book to readers. To earn $2.00 per sale on an e-book with an eight-megabyte file, you'll need to list your book for at least $4.48.

With that in mind, you may think of listing your e-book for the more common price of $4.49 or $4.99. But if most comparable e-books in your chosen categories are listed for $2.99 or $3.99, you'll likely struggle to sell copies of your e-book at $4.00 or above. So do your research on list prices, adjust your expectations when necessary, and price your book in a way that maximizes your income at a price point your ideal readers will be willing to pay.

After determining the list price for your primary marketplace, you can set individual list prices for global marketplaces on applicable platforms (e.g., Amazon KDP, Google Play, Kobo Writing Life). Don't worry if you're intimidated by the idea of pricing your book in a foreign currency. Most platforms offer automatic calculations for global list prices based on the price you set for your primary marketplace. Adjust these prices as needed to maximize marketability. For example, if Amazon KDP suggests listing your book for £2.88 in their United Kingdom marketplace, you may want to round up to the more typical price of £2.99.

When creating an e-book listing in Amazon KDP, you might encounter the option to activate the Kindle Book Lending feature, which allows a customer to share their digital copy of your book with a family member or friend for fourteen days. Allowing Kindle Book Lending is a requirement if you want to receive Amazon KDP's 70 percent royalty rate, but I recommend enabling this option anyway. It might seem like you're allowing someone to read your book for "free," but Kindle Book Lending is no different from someone sharing a physical copy of your book with a friend. And the more people who read your books, the more your readership (and future sales!) will grow.

With your pricing set, you've finished entering all the information needed to create your book's listings. If you aren't ready to publish your book yet, you can save your listing as a draft.

And if you'd like to preview your book before publishing, you can order printed proof copies or review a digital proof. Ordering proof copies is also a great way to stock up on ARCs to send as part of your prelaunch marketing efforts.

When you're ready to publish, simply click the appropriate Publish button. As long as the distributor or aggregator approves your files and metadata, your book should be available for sale on your platform(s) of choice within seventy-two hours. Congratulations, writer!

13

PRODUCING AN AUDIOBOOK

Given the ease of listening during life's unhurried moments, it's no wonder that audiobooks are increasing in popularity among readers. Some studies project that audiobooks will outsell e-books—the world's best-selling book format—over the next few years. But is it possible for independent authors to take advantage of this growing market by self-publishing audio editions of their books? Absolutely!

Online audiobook distributors like Amazon's Audiobook Creation Exchange (ACX), Kobo Writing Life, and Findaway Voices make it easy to distribute self-published audiobooks to readers around the globe. However, audiobooks can be expensive to produce. To determine whether offering an audio edition of your book is right for you, let's explore the major aspects of audiobook production and the potential costs involved. Once again, all prices are listed in US dollars.

Production Aspect 1: Narration

Some authors choose to narrate their own audiobooks. Others hire professional narrators to complete this work for them.

Determining who will narrate your audiobook is a decision that shouldn't be made lightly.

Audio narration is skilled work that can be difficult and time-consuming, and it often requires a significant amount of performance ability. Even if you have experience with skills like breath modulation, voice acting, and enunciation, you might not be the right narrator for your book. For example, if you've written a novel that features a protagonist whose gender or nationality is different from yours, you might leave readers confused or befuddled should you choose to narrate your book.

In addition, recording an audiobook can be exhausting. An hour of finished audio can take up to twice as long to record due to narration mistakes and short breaks needed to maintain the clarity and consistency of the narration. Narrating also requires steady focus and a constant high level of energy that can be physically draining.

If you're interested in narrating your audiobook, you'll also want to consider the time commitment. Audiobooks are typically recorded in one- to two-hour sessions to preserve the narrator's voice and ensure the best-quality narration. This means that recording a full-length audiobook (i.e., four or more hours) can take weeks, if not months.

The alternative to self-narrating your audiobook is to commission a professional narrator. You can do so through a distributor such as ACX or an online freelance marketplace such as Fiverr, Reedsy, or Voices. Most narrators work for a flat per-finished-hour (PFH) rate (since narrators charge *per finished hour* of audio), which accounts for the work of both recording and engineering (i.e., editing and mastering) the narration. PFH rates for audiobook narration typically cost between $150 and $300, though some may start as low as $50 or climb over $400.

As with any part of the book production process, you tend to get what you pay for. To estimate the cost of hiring a narrator, divide your book's total word count by 9,500—the average number of words per hour in a finished audiobook—then multiply that number by your PFH rate of choice. For example, if you've written a 75,000-word novel and would like to hire a narrator who charges $225 PFH, expect the narration to cost approximately $1,777.50. Here's the math:

75,000 total words / 9,500 words per hour = 7.9 hours of audio
7.9 hours × $225 PFH = $1,777.50

If you can't afford to hire a professional narrator but don't want to record your book yourself, don't give up just yet. Several options are still available to you, depending on your budget.

First, you may want to take advantage of ACX's Royalty Share program. With this option, a narrator will record your audiobook for "free" in exchange for a 50 percent share of the audiobook royalties you earn over seven years. To pursue this option, you'll need to publish your audiobook exclusively through ACX for the duration of the seven-year contract to ensure that your narrator receives their full 50 percent share of royalties.

While ACX's Royalty Share program is great for authors who otherwise can't afford to produce an audiobook, the downside is that most experienced audiobook narrators don't take on split royalty contracts. There's simply no guarantee that the audiobook will sell well, which means the narrator might never receive the royalties needed to adequately compensate them for their work. The narrators who are most likely to agree to a split royalty contract are those who are new to the field and looking to establish their portfolios—and, therefore, they may lack the experience needed to narrate a fantastic audiobook. That said, with a little time and effort, you might find exceptions to the rule.

If you're struggling to find a great narrator who's willing to take on a split royalty contract, you may have better luck with a hybrid package. This type of narration contract marries a royalty split with an up-front payment, lessening the narrator's financial risk while making professional narration more afford-able for the author.

Both ACX and Findaway Voices offer narration hybrid packages. With ACX, authors and narrators negotiate a reduced PFH rate that's paid up front while agreeing to a fifty-fifty royalty split. There is still a seven-year contract for the royalty share, and you'll still need to remain exclusive with ACX during that time. However, the hybrid deal increases your chances of commissioning a great narrator without breaking the bank.

Findaway Voices offers a similar package through their Voices Share program, where an author can hire a narrator for half the usual PFH rate by agreeing to share 20 percent of their royalties with the narrator over ten years. As with ACX, you'll need to publish your audiobook exclusively with Find-away Voices to participate in the Voices Share program. But since Findaway Voices is an aggregator and not a direct distributor, you aren't limited to offering your audiobook solely through Amazon and Audible. Instead, you can distribute your audiobook to dozens of marketplaces and library apps around the world, including Amazon and Audi-ble. You can also buy your way out of a Voices Share contract at any time. This is a great option, especially if your audiobook income takes off.

Production Aspect 2: Recording

If you're hiring a professional narrator for your audiobook, you don't need to worry about the recording process. The narrator will handle that aspect of audiobook production for you. But if you're interested in self-narrating your audiobook, you'll need to decide where you'll record the audio. Unless you're lucky enough to have a home studio, two options are available to you.

First, you can create a small recording setup at home in a carpeted room that's free of echo and significant external noise (e.g., traffic, appliance hums, loud children). You'll also need a good-quality microphone, a pop filter to blunt the harsher vocal sounds that can spike audio levels, and audio production software. A decent microphone—such as my personal favorite, the Blue Yeti—typically costs between $50 and $200, while pop filters are often less than $20. You can also download a quality piece of audio production software, such as Audacity, for free.

The alternative to home recording is to rent time at a local recording studio. This can cost anywhere between several hundred and several thousand dollars depending on the studio's rates, as well as whether you hire an audio technician to engineer the raw audio files for you.

Production Aspect 3: Engineering

If you commission a narrator to record your audiobook, the expense of audio engineering is included in the PFH rate, split royalty contract, or hybrid deal. However, if you've elected to self-narrate your audiobook, you'll need to decide who will engineer your raw audio files.

If you're experienced with audio production and aren't intimidated by distributors' strict lists of audio requirements, you can use an audio software of choice to self-engineer your audiobook files. Alternatively, you can hire an audio engineer to prepare your files for you.

If you've rented studio time to record your audiobook, the studio may provide editing and mastering services. Otherwise, your best option is to hire a freelance audio engineer through an online marketplace like Upwork or Fiverr, where rates for this type of work typically fall between $25 and $100 per hour.

(Note that this is per hour of work, not per finished hour of audio.) Depending on the engineer's rate and the length of your raw audio files, expect to pay between $300 and $800 to hire an audio engineer to edit and prepare a 75,000-word audiobook for distribution.

Production Aspect 4: Cover Design

In addition to the expense of producing your audiobook files, you'll need to procure a cover for your audiobook. Audiobook covers are typically a square design (3200 × 3200 pixels) that mimics the book's print and digital cover for continuity.

Fortunately, commissioning this type of cover design isn't expensive. Most book design companies and freelance cover designers will happily bundle the cost of multiple cover formats into one affordable package. However, if you've already purchased your print and e-book cover designs, expect to pay between $50 and $150 to commission a separate audiobook cover.

Exploring Audiobook Distribution Options

As I previously mentioned, the three most popular audiobook distribution platforms are ACX, Findaway Voices, and Kobo Writing Life.

ACX is Amazon's direct distribution platform for audiobooks, as well as a marketplace connecting rights holders such as indie authors with "producers" who narrate and engineer professional audiobooks. ACX is currently available to authors living in the United States, Canada, the United Kingdom, and Ireland. Publishing an audiobook through ACX is a great option for authors looking to maximize their royalties while taking advantage of the popularity of Amazon's Audible audiobook subscription service and marketplace.

Unfortunately, authors who publish with ACX don't get to set the prices of their audiobooks. Instead, ACX calculates the price of an audiobook based on its length. This price can then change at any time depending on Audible promotions and changes in the ACX pricing algorithm. For many reasons, this isn't an ideal reality for most authors—primarily because ACX tends to overprice audiobooks (e.g., $20 to $50) to encourage listeners to subscribe to Audible, wherein audiobook prices are more affordable. ACX does offer occasional discounts for non-Audible listeners, but their lofty retail prices and manipulative pricing model can be displeasing to many customers.

If you'd prefer not to place all of your eggs in Amazon's basket, you're in luck. The audiobook aggregator Findaway Voices boasts the tagline "Take Back Your Freedom" to highlight the many features their platform affords independent authors, including the ability to set the price of their audiobooks for retail and library distribution. Most Findaway Voices features are available to authors worldwide, and publishing with Findaway Voices allows you to sell your audiobook through more than forty global retailers. Other features include promotional pricing and the ability to sell directly to your readers through the Authors Direct app.

Finally, you may want to list your audiobook with Kobo Writing Life, the direct distribution platform I mentioned in chapter 11. Uploading with Kobo Writing Life allows you to maximize royalties earned for sales made through Kobo.com. You can also use the platform to list your audiobook with Kobo's sister company, OverDrive, which distributes digital books to libraries around the world, as well as to expanded distribution options like Walmart's online marketplace. While you can reach these same markets through Findaway Voices, Kobo Writing Life's advanced promotion opportunities and higher royalty rates make it worthwhile to upload to Kobo Writing Life directly.

In addition, you may want to explore up-and-coming platforms such as Lantern Audio and Author's Republic. These platforms aren't as well established as the others, so it's difficult for me to recommend them. However, they appear to be growing in popularity and are worth considering if you're dissatisfied with the options discussed earlier.

Should You Go Wide or Stay Exclusive with Audio?

As with print and e-book publishing, you'll need to decide whether you'd like to go wide or publish your audiobook exclusively through ACX.

While I made no recommendations earlier for print and e-book publishing, I do recommend going wide with audiobook distribution. By going wide, you'll earn a decreased royalty rate on books sold through Amazon and Audible. However, this might not pose as devastating a blow to your audiobook revenue as you might expect. While Amazon still dominates print and e-book markets, they don't have nearly as strong a hold on audiobook sales thanks to the success of retailers like Kobo, Google Play, and Chirp. This means you're likely to earn a higher income by going wide with audio.

Notice that I didn't mention publishing exclusively with Findaway Voices. If you sign a split royalty contract through their Voices Share program, technically, you'll need to publish exclusively through Findaway Voices for the duration of that contract. But remember that Findaway Voices is an audiobook aggregator, not a direct distribution platform. This means that you can cultivate a wide range of income streams by selling your audiobook through dozens of online marketplaces *regardless* of whether you publish exclusively with Findaway Voices. Hello, self-publishing freedom!

No matter which distribution option you choose, self-publishing an audiobook is a fantastic way to get your book

into the hands of the millions of readers who enjoy listening to their favorite books and stories. And with the audiobook market expanding at its current rate, it might not be long before your audiobook income streams rival the profit you earn from paperback and e-book editions of your book.

PART III

LAUNCHING AND MARKETING YOUR BOOK

14

AN INTRODUCTION TO EFFECTIVE BOOK MARKETING

That's right, my friend. The time has come for us to talk about marketing.

Unfortunately, earning a living as an indie author isn't as simple as clicking the Publish button and watching book sales roll in. If you want to profit from your published work, marketing is an essential act. The good news is that book promotion doesn't have to be the creativity-killing time suck that many writers fear it to be. Nor should marketing feel dirty, demanding, or downright draining. In truth, there's no reason why your marketing efforts can't be as enjoyable and fulfilling as the writing process itself—or close enough to it.

So what's the secret to marketing without losing your mind? Marketing with your heart instead.

Does that sound silly? Well, hear me out.

The most effective and enjoyable book marketing tactics aren't forms of self-promotion—they're acts of service. By writing a book, you've created a valuable piece of media. Maybe you've written a self-help guide to help readers process grief or take control of their health, a literary novel or poetry collection that will engage readers' minds with contemplative thoughts about the human condition, or an immersive alien space thriller that will transport readers out of this world for a few hours of fun. Whatever the case, your book holds incredible power.

The power to shape someone's worldview.

The power to educate or inspire.

The power to bring someone joy.

Should you fail to promote your work, you'll rob readers of its power. You'll withhold the opportunity for them to fall in love with your book, share it with friends, and call it their new favorite read. Do you see how, in this light, book marketing is an act of service? How the primary purpose of promotion is to get your book into the hands of your ideal readers?

If this language doesn't resonate with you, ask yourself why. Because if you don't believe in your book's power and purpose, you're already undermining your success as an indie author. It might not be difficult to think of your book as important if you write within a niche that society considers worthy of merit, such as literary fiction or biography. But your work isn't any less valuable if you write lighthearted fluff or humor books with silly sketches. Life is hard, and readers need an escape. "The direction of escape is toward freedom," wrote renowned author Ursula K. Le Guin in *No Time to Spare*, addressing society's often dismissive attitude toward fantasy fiction. "So what is 'escapism' an accusation of?" Believe that your book matters, and you'll find far greater success in your marketing endeavors.

All the same, there's nothing wrong with wanting to profit from your published work. Your books are both intrinsically *and* monetarily valuable, and you deserve to be paid for your labor. Marketing can help you achieve this. Nevertheless, framing marketing as an act of service first and foremost is key to avoiding distasteful and demanding promotion tactics. Offer value to readers, and they'll return the favor. But demand value the second you have their attention, and you'll never make a dime.

At this point, you might be wondering what a reader-centric approach to book marketing looks like. There's no easy answer to this question—and that's a good thing. Every author is unique. Their personalities, interests, and schedules can vary wildly. So can the nature of their books. If there were only one or two successful book marketing strategies, few authors would find pleasure in promoting their work. Fortunately, there are *lots* of ways to successfully market a book with readers in mind. This means that you'll likely find an approach to self-promotion that will be effective and enjoyable for you.

The Five Main Types of Book Marketing

Indie authors have used countless strategies to get their books into the hands of readers, and new book marketing tactics emerge each day as technology (and the indie author industry) evolves. Given that *Self-Publishing Simplified* is a guide to producing and publishing a profitable book, I'd be remiss not to discuss book marketing to some degree. However, the most lucrative book marketing techniques have changed many times since digital and POD distribution services first made their debut in the mid-2000s. Given the fickle nature of book marketing in the internet age, my intent in part 3 of this book isn't to offer a comprehensive view of all of the strategies available to you. Instead, I'll focus on the most popular and effective book marketing techniques that indie authors have used with relative consistency over the last two decades.

Generally speaking, these techniques can be sorted into five main types of book marketing:

1. **Content Marketing:** Building and maintaining a

secondary body of work designed to attract one's ideal readers.

2. **Email Marketing:** Cultivating and connecting with an email list of ideal readers to whom one can pitch their work.

3. **Paid Advertising:** Using direct advertising campaigns on popular platforms to actively promote one's books to readers.

4. **Visibility Marketing:** Collaborating and networking with fellow creators with the intent to expand one's reach.

5. **Spike Marketing:** Using book launch strategies and limited-time price drops to temporarily spike book sales.

If you'd like to learn more about each of these five types of book marketing, you're in luck. We'll explore each one in dedicated chapters throughout this third part of the book.

You may have noticed that I didn't mention one of the most popular forms of modern promotion: social media marketing. This wasn't a mistake. Social media is a fantastic marketing tool that authors can use to complete some of the main types of book marketing, especially content marketing, paid advertising, and visibility marketing. Social media can also play a lesser role in your email and spike marketing strategies. This versatility is what makes social media such an important cornerstone of most authors' platforms, and in the upcoming chapters, we'll discuss many of the ways you can use social media to expand your reach and revenue.

Speaking of reach and revenue, it's important to note that "book marketing" can comprise several key activities that help authors thrive in their publishing journeys. These activities include promotion resulting in direct book sales as well as author platform development strategies that help authors expand and connect with their readership. This means that some book marketing strategies don't translate into immediate income. Instead, they're designed to help you develop a larger platform from which you can sell your books for years to come. Understanding what each book marketing method can help you achieve is therefore key to crafting and implementing a plan for long-term self-publishing success.

Where Do You Fall on the Book Marketing Spectrum?

Most book marketing strategies fall within the bounds of the "push versus pull" marketing spectrum, which can also be described as "direct versus community" marketing.

Push marketing consists of paid advertising and spike marketing opportunities designed to "push" one's product in front of customers. These strategies often result in an immediate boost in income. They also take less time to implement and maintain than community-based marketing strategies, which makes push marketing a great option for indie authors with busy production schedules. Some high-volume authors rely solely on push marketing campaigns for promotion, as do many authors who maintain multiple platforms for various types of work. However, push marketing campaigns consist primarily of short-term promotion strategies. Without pairing push marketing with some form of readership engagement (e.g., an email list), authors may struggle to promote new releases to their existing readership.

On the opposite end of the spectrum is **pull marketing**, which consists of strategies designed to attract and maintain customers' ongoing interest. Most content marketing, email marketing, and visibility marketing opportunities fall into this area. For authors, pull marketing is all about building and maintaining an engaged readership. Many pull marketing strategies don't result in an immediate boost in book sales.

Instead, authors who use pull marketing see slow but steady growth in their reach and revenue. Spike marketing strategies and paid advertising campaigns also tend to prove more lucrative for authors with engaged readerships, as they can promote new books or sales directly to existing readers.

Authors who publish less frequently often find great success with pull marketing strategies that help them keep readers engaged between launches. Pull marketing can also help nonfiction authors establish the credibility they need to successfully sell their books. However, many pull marketing strategies can be time-consuming. This is especially true for authors who choose to build a secondary body of work, such as a blog or podcast, to attract their ideal readers. Nevertheless, these strategies can prove worthwhile for many authors as developing an engaged readership can help one find financial stability amid the turbulence of an ever-shifting industry.

While many authors have found financial success by focusing on one end of the spectrum or the other, most indie authors thrive by employing both push and pull marketing strategies. Some types of marketing even allow authors to engage in both endeavors at once. Consider email marketing, for example. If an author offers valuable free content to readers who sign up for their email list, they're attempting to *pull* readers in. That same author can then promote a limited-time price drop to their email list to *push* readers to make a purchase.

So, as an author, where do you fall on the "push versus pull" marketing spectrum? Consider your chosen business model, creative niche, and definition of publishing success. If you write high-volume fiction, employing paid advertising campaigns as your primary form of marketing will help protect your valuable writing time. Alternatively, if your definition of publishing success includes daily interactions with adoring readers, community-based marketing techniques are likely right for you. All things considered, it's never a bad idea to experiment with both push and pull marketing strategies to identify which one you find most effective and enjoyable. The remaining chapters of this book can help you determine where to start.

Prerequisites for Successful Book Marketing

If you've been paying close attention, you'll remember that we've already discussed several aspects of book marketing in parts 1 and 2 of this book. Consider the importance of defining your creative niche, for starters. Without a clear understanding of what you write and who you write for, you'll struggle to sell copies of your books. We've also discussed the importance of crafting effective book titles, cover designs, and listing descriptions. Each of these elements works in tandem to attract the attention of readers and secure sales. In fact, these elements are so essential to effective book marketing that many indie authors choose to overhaul them should their books undersell.

As we gear up to discuss additional book marketing techniques, it's important to consider your budget. While most marketing strategies don't require ongoing expenses, some do involve start-up costs. For instance, you can't launch a website without paying for a website host and domain name. Nor can you launch a podcast or run a YouTube channel without decent starter equipment (or, at the very least, a high-quality smartphone). It's also helpful to have a small budget for paid advertising campaigns, which can help you secure early sales.

If you're hesitant to set aside a budget for book marketing, try to view this money as an *investment* in your writing career rather than an *expense*. Though you might not see an immediate return on that investment, especially in the early days of your publishing journey, there's no denying that all financially successful indie authors know how to leverage marketing strategies to drastically increase their reach and revenue. So start small, and be patient. As you continue to develop your platform and promote your books, you *will* see undeniable growth in your sales and readership—growth that will compound tenfold over time and that wouldn't be possible without an early investment in your writing career.

It can be difficult to consider the many years it may take to develop a sizable author platform and income. I've been there myself; in many ways, I'm still in the early days of my publishing journey. Remember that, as independent authors, we're in this for the long haul. To fortify yourself for the road ahead, you must adopt the indie author mindset discussed in chapter 6. You must be willing to think long term, to commit to the journey, and to use doubts and failures as springboards for growth as you trek toward your definition of publishing success, all while enjoying every step along the way. No one skips this journey. Even the authors whose debut books enjoy extraordinary success aren't guaranteed to maintain their good fortune over time. It takes more than a lucky break to sustain a thriving career in any field.

The good news is that small successes often compound. As a personal finance geek, I know that the small contributions I make to my retirement accounts today hold the power to make me a millionaire thirty-odd years down the road. It might take me a decade or more to reach a net worth of $100,000, but the power of compound interest will make each subsequent $100,000 easier to earn. This same principle is true for your marketing efforts. It might take a year to sell the first 1,000 copies of your book—or even the first 100 copies. But every reader who purchases your book holds the power to share it with their family, friends, and social media followers, as well as leave valuable ratings and reviews on your listings. Thus, one sale becomes three, which becomes ten. Before you know it, you're well on your way to achieving your personal definition of publishing success.

See how your early marketing efforts can compound, even when they might feel fruitless at first? This is why it's so important to persist when laying the groundwork for all the fantastic growth you'll experience in your writing life. It may take time to realize the effects of compound growth, but I promise that the wait will be worth your while.

If you're just getting started in your publishing journey, establishing your author platform is the most important step you can take toward setting yourself up for a successful writing life. Without a platform, you have nothing to market, no readers to reach, and no profit to enjoy. For this reason, the next chapter will guide you through establishing and developing your author platform step-by-step.

15

ESTABLISHING YOUR AUTHOR PLATFORM

Many activities can help you grow your readership and market your work as an author. But a readership isn't an author platform in and of itself, and neither is your marketing effort.

Earlier in the book, I defined an author platform as an author's capacity for generating revenue as determined by the visibility and credibility of their work. The word *capacity* implies action. If you reach out to your readers tomorrow with an announcement that immediately boosts your book sales, you've built an effective author platform—the foundation of a creative career that makes all other book marketing efforts possible. Establishing and developing a platform is, therefore, key to your ability to reach readers and sell more books.

In chapter 4, I briefly touched on the four cornerstones of an effective modern author platform:

1. A backlist
2. A social media presence
3. An author website
4. An email list

As with most things in life, there are exceptions to this rule. Some indie authors effectively market their work without the benefit of a social media presence, website, or email list—most often through the heavy use of paid ads. However, think of each cornerstone of an author's platform as a leg on a chair. Some authors have no trouble selling their work while standing on a three-legged stool, but most can't balance on stilts (or a pogo stick!) for long. Publishing and marketing trends are bound to change over time. The best way to withstand industry turbulence and achieve long-term success as an indie author is to build a stable, diversified author platform from the start.

With that in mind, let's look at how you can establish and develop each cornerstone of your author platform.

Cornerstone 1: Your Backlist

As an author, you understand that your backlist is the most important aspect of your platform. Published books, especially those with positive ratings and reviews, provide the social proof and credibility that many readers need to take a chance on a new author. The readers who enjoy your earlier books are also the most likely people to continue buying from you as you write and release new work. That's why I encourage new authors—especially those who would like to write and publish books for a living—to invest the bulk of their time and energy into building their backlist as their primary platform development strategy. Remember this old publishing mantra: "Nothing sells your first book better than your second."

Beyond writing new books, the key to harnessing your backlist as a platform development tool lies in honoring your creative niche. If you follow your debut contemporary romance with a psychological horror novel, your second published book will do little to help sell your first. If anything, your horror novel might lead fewer readers to purchase your contemporary romance. Remember that most readers aren't just searching for their next great read. They're on the lookout for authors who can provide them with great reads for years to come. By publishing books in unrelated genres under the same name, you undermine your potential to keep readers coming back for more by failing to establish what they can expect from your work.

If you plan to publish in multiple genres or subgenres, review the discussion in chapter 5. By identifying a common creative thread that weaves through all of your work, you increase your chances of successfully publishing books in multiple genres under one author name. Otherwise, develop separate platforms to avoid reader confusion and better market your work.

One way to craft a backlist designed for financial success is to publish a series. Most readers love discovering a new book series, since it will provide several days or weeks of great reading material. In turn, publishing a series can boost your book sales as readers return to purchase multiple installments.

Don't worry if you aren't interested in writing a traditional fiction book series where readers must consume every installment to enjoy the full scope of the story, though. A series of related stand-alone books hold the same power. For example, many romance readers enjoy series that follow a group of friends or siblings as their individual love stories unfold. Similarly, many mystery readers enjoy series where the detective protagonist solves a new murder in each book. Nonfiction authors can also take advantage of the power of a book series by writing closely related books. For example, a cookbook author may write a series of books that feature gluten-free snacks, meals, and desserts. Alternatively, a popular science author could publish a series on different areas of interest within the field of astronomy.

Authors who publish series or related books can also boost

their revenue by marketing their books as box sets, allowing readers to purchase multiple books at a more cost-effective price. You might think that solely offering individual books—which, cumulatively, would have a higher profit margin—would be the smarter business move, but the opposite is true. Offering a box set encourages readers to make a larger purchase up front rather than requiring them to return over a series of weeks or months to purchase individual books. Readers also love a deal, which is why many indie authors report that their box sets generate greater revenue than any of their book listings.

Cornerstone 2: Social Media

Social media is a powerful platform cornerstone because it offers authors a way to reach and connect with readers in their everyday lives. After all, most of us spend a good portion of our time scrolling through social media feeds, right? Despite their love for books, readers are no exception. In fact, there are massive reading communities on nearly every social network, including Facebook, Twitter, Instagram, YouTube, Reddit, and TikTok.

Connecting with readers through social networking is important for several reasons. First, readers enjoy buying books from authors they know and love, and social media provides an excellent opportunity to build this type of relationship with readers and become more than just a shiny headshot in an author bio. Second, readers are more likely to stay in touch with an author's career—and purchase their new books—when they have an easy way to follow the author online. For that purpose, social media can be a fantastic tool. Finally, many readers need repeated exposure to a book before they'll decide to buy it. A social presence therefore gives authors an additional channel for keeping their books fresh in the minds of readers.

Speaking of which, authors can use their social media presence to engage in or support nearly all of their book marketing efforts. We'll discuss various strategies in detail over the next several chapters, so stay tuned.

All things considered, getting started on social media can undoubtedly feel overwhelming. Which platforms should you join? What should you post? How can you use different marketing tactics to grow your following? These are all great questions to ask.

When getting started on social media, start small. Running a successful social media presence can be incredibly time-consuming if you don't act with clarity and intention. To do this, create accounts on just one or two networks where your ideal readers hang out, especially if you already enjoy using those networks in your personal life. Teen and YA readers tend to have a larger presence on platforms like YouTube, Instagram, and TikTok, while older adults are more present on Facebook. Meanwhile, Reddit has individual forums (called *subreddits*) for nearly every type of reader. However, you may have a tougher time using Reddit as a marketing tool given common subreddit rules that ban self-promotion.

Another factor to consider when choosing which social media network(s) you'll use to establish your social presence is paid advertising. While most social networks offer paid advertising opportunities, Facebook Ads is by far the most effective social advertising network for authors. If your readers are on Facebook (and there's a darn good chance they are), you may want to create a Facebook author page to ensure that you can use the site's robust ad network.

And if you don't enjoy using social media in your personal life? Then you may hesitate when it comes to creating a professional social presence. Being an extreme introvert, I understand. I often find social media draining, and I don't use social networks in my personal life beyond watching the occasional YouTube video. Nevertheless, when I first launched my online business, I felt the pressure to maintain a presence on all the major social networks. In the words of Bilbo Baggins, this left me feeling "like butter scraped over too much bread." It wasn't until June 2020 that I scaled things back, maintaining a social media presence solely on Instagram. And after several months of trial and error, I discovered a strategy for engaging on social media that I actually enjoyed. Find that strategy for yourself, and you'll find your social media work much more effective and sustainable.

Also, remember that you're only one person. As an author, you likely won't encounter much success with building meaningful connections with readers if you spread yourself too thin across social media. You won't grow the reach of your platform by showing up briefly and inconsistently in as many places as possible. Instead, you'll reach your readers by being present, by carving out time to interact and engage in the one or two places that matter most.

As for what to post on social media, check out the content ideas I share in chapter 17. These ideas are intended for use in the emails you'd send to subscribers in your mailing list, but they also apply to any avenue you use to engage with readers. Plus, it doesn't hurt to follow a few of your favorite authors to glean content ideas. Imitation is the sincerest form of flattery.

Finally, you may be eager to learn how to grow your social media following. Each platform will have its own best practices. But generally speaking, the best plan is to create high-value content that appeals to your ideal reader no matter which network(s) you use. Many of the tips I share in chapter 16 can help you achieve this goal.

Cornerstone 3: An Author Website

To succeed in the business of writing and selling books, you'll need an online headquarters—a place readers can visit to learn everything they want to know about who you are, what you write, and where they can purchase your books. Knowing this, some authors create Facebook Pages or focus on padding out their Amazon Author Central profile. However, these platforms are limited in their scope. There are plenty of readers who don't use Facebook or purchase books through Amazon. Relying solely on these two platforms also leaves you vulnerable to unwelcome policy and interface changes. With a website, you remain fully in charge of how you present yourself to readers around the world and ensure that any reader with internet access can learn more about you and your books.

The most effective author websites are simple and professional. They establish your credibility as an author, communicate necessary information to readers, and serve as the foundation of your online book marketing efforts by encouraging readers to subscribe to your email list and follow you on social media. Even so, every author's website will be unique. The information an author chooses to include on their site will depend on the genre(s) they write, who they write for, and how experienced they are in their writing career.

Every author website should include these six key types of content.

Content Type 1: A Home Page

When readers type your website address into their internet browser, your home page will be the first thing they see. To make a positive first impression, avoid stuffing this page with a lengthy author bio or book descriptions. Instead, use your home page to introduce readers to who you are and what you write, then redirect them to pages where they can learn more, such as an "About the Author" page, individual book pages, or an email subscription page.

Content Type 2: An "About the Author" Page

Your "About the Author" page is where you'll tell readers more about who you are and what you write. However, this page isn't really about you—it's about your readers. An effective "About the Author" page encourages readers to pick up your books by explaining what makes your work unique. While it's OK to share a few key details about your life (e.g., where you live, whether you have kids, what hobbies you enjoy), consider skipping a list of fun facts about yourself in favor of detailing how you can serve your readers.

In addition to your bio and a detailed introduction to your work, your "About the Author" page should include your author photo. Over time, you may want to add links to interviews, articles, or book reviews that lend credibility to your status as a published author.

Content Type 3: Book Description Pages

It should come as no surprise that you should talk about your published books on your author website. Most authors choose to create one main page that provides an overview of their published books, which then links to pages where readers can learn more about each book individually.

Individual book pages should include the book's cover, listing description, and links to where the book can be purchased online. You may also want to include excerpts from book reviews, author blurbs, and other notable praise.

Content Type 4: A "Contact" Page

Remember to give readers a way to get in touch with you through your author website. Ideally, your "Contact" page should include an easy email form, though simply listing your email address is acceptable. By extension, your public email address should be professional and unique to your creative work. If possible, set up an email address using your **domain name** (i.e., your website's unique web address), such as author-name@authorwebsite.com. If you can't create an email address using your domain name, consider creating a Gmail account using your author name instead.

In addition to a contact form or email address, you may want to include a list of frequently asked questions on your contact page. These FAQs should highlight important information such as where readers can purchase your books and when you plan to launch your next release.

Content Type 5: Social Media Links

If you maintain a social media presence for your creative work, you'll want to include links to your accounts on your website. Most authors choose to include social links in their website's header and footer. Some also include social links on their "About the Author" page, their "Contact" page, or their website's sidebar.

Content Type 6: A Newsletter Subscription Page

An author's email list is their direct line of contact to their core readership. Including an easy newsletter subscription page on your website is one of many ways to encourage readers to sign up for your email list.

Should You Include a Blog on Your Author Website?

You may have noticed that I didn't mention anything about blogging on your author website—and for good reason. Many authors hesitate to build their websites out of fear that creating content for a blog will take valuable time away from their book-writing efforts. They're not wrong. Blogs can be incredibly time-consuming to maintain with consistency, and content marketing is only one of many ways to develop your reach and readership as an author. You may want to read chapter 16, which addresses content marketing in detail, before deciding whether to add a blog to your author website.

How Do You Set Up an Author Website?

Creating an author website may seem like a huge task that involves significant technical know-how, but that doesn't have to be the case. In fact, most authors can set up a website in one quick and (relatively) painless weekend by working through the following steps.

Step 1: Choose a Web Host and Website Builder

To create a website, you'll first need to choose a **web host** (i.e., a company that stores your site files on its servers and connects them to the internet) and a **website builder** (i.e., the platform you'll use to create your site). Don't worry if this sounds complicated. Many companies, including Squarespace and Wix, offer both services in one easy package.

Step 2: Purchase a Domain Name

A domain name is your website's unique web address (e.g., well-storied.com). You can purchase a domain name through most website building and hosting companies, Squarespace and Wix included. Be sure to choose a domain name that's simple and professional, preferably one that features your author name. Consider a domain name that follows one of these formats:

- authorname.com
- firstname-lastname.com
- authornamebooks.com
- worldofauthorname.com
- authornameromances.com

Avoid choosing a domain name that centers on the title of your debut book or series, since you'll likely publish more books down the road. The last thing you want to do is switch domain names *after* establishing your author platform. If you're having trouble finding an appropriate domain name that's available with a .com ending, consider .net or .co instead.

Step 3: Design Your Website

Quality design is key to your site's credibility and readability. Fortunately, you don't need to hire a professional designer to create a site for you. Instead, you can create a beautiful site design yourself using an editable, premade template provided by your website builder. If you decide to tweak your template, be sure to keep your author brand in mind. We'll talk more about this concept in a moment. For now, know that you won't sell many horror novels with a bright pink website design.

Step 4: Add Your Content

You already know the types of content to include on your site. Now's the time to add that information. Bear in mind that professional copy (i.e., text) is key to your site's credibility and success as a marketing tool. Keeping things professional doesn't mean sanitizing your tone, but it does mean that every word on your site should serve a purpose. Also, remember to proofread your content. A website riddled with typos will do little to encourage readers to buy your book.

Step 5: Launch Your Site

With your website design and content complete, it's time to share your author website with the world. Consider adding your website link to your social media bios, in the back matter of your published books, and in your email footer—anywhere readers are likely to look to learn more about who you are and what you write.

Cornerstone 4: An Email List

An email list is the most effective way to contact your core readership directly. Social media can help with this to a degree, but the algorithms will rarely show all of your posts to everyone who follows you. Therefore, if you want to ensure that your ideal readers get your message when you reach out to them, you'll need a more direct line of contact. This is where an email list comes into play.

If you reach out to your core readership tomorrow with an announcement that immediately boosts your book sales, you'll know you've built an effective author platform. Consistently connecting with your readers is therefore key to maintaining their attention in between book releases, when readers might otherwise forget to follow your publishing journey. Building an email list is also a way to ensure that you'll still have a way to sell books even if one or more distribution platforms are no longer available to you. In that sense, an email list offers indie authors true independence from industry gatekeepers and regulators.

Additionally, an email list is the most accurate way to gauge the size of your readership. In 2021, I led an online workshop called "Your First 100 Readers," where I taught strategies authors can use to develop their email lists (many of which we'll cover in this section). During that workshop, I explained that an author's email list might not include every reader who actively follows their work, but it does offer a more accurate figure than social media numbers or sales totals can provide. If every author's social media followers purchased their books, authors as a whole would be far wealthier than they are. As for sales figures, a single purchase is no indication that a reader will purchase more of an author's books. An email list, on the other hand, is rarely something that readers subscribe to unless they genuinely want to follow the author's journey. That's why I encouraged workshop attendees to view their first 100 email subscribers as their first 100 readers.

With that in mind, how do you get your email list up and running? The process is simple.

Step 1: Choose an Email Marketing Service

An email marketing service is a special type of email service provider that allows you to build and contact a list of email subscribers. Mailchimp and MailerLite are great options for new authors because both allow you to build a list of at least 1,000 subscribers for free. For a bigger list, you may want to look into ConvertKit. Whatever service you choose, ensure that it has core features like email automation and subscriber segmenting, both of which you'll need to make full use of the marketing strategies we'll discuss throughout the rest of this book.

Step 2: Build a Sign-Up Form

After creating an account with your email marketing service of choice, it's time to build a sign-up form to capture your readers' email addresses. Any good email marketing service will make this process easy and intuitive. Once your form is complete, embed it on your author website to begin capturing email addresses.

If you're eager to learn more about how to develop your email list, the types of content to send to your subscribers, and how to effectively promote your books via email, stay tuned. We'll cover the topic of email marketing in depth in chapter 17.

When Should You Begin Building Your Platform?

Now you know how to establish each of the four cornerstones of a modern author platform. But when should you get your platform off the ground? If you've been a member of the online writing community for a while, you've probably heard some authors say that it's never too early to begin building your author platform. I agree with this—to an extent. Most expository nonfiction authors need the credibility of an established platform to sell books. In part, an author platform is the proof of credibility that encourages readers to purchase your work. But if you're a regular Joe Schmo with no credentials or online following, you'll struggle to convince readers to buy your informational nonfiction book. You simply don't have the qualifications to impart business advice or teach the basics of neuroscience.

On the flip side, novelists and creative nonfiction authors (e.g., memoirists, poets) don't need to prove that they're qualified to write their books. Their credibility comes largely from the quality of the work itself. That's why the most important step that novelists and creative nonfiction authors can take to establish their platforms is to publish their debut books.

Yes, there's a good case to be made for developing other aspects of your author platform *before* publishing, regardless of what you write. It never hurts to have a small following so you can market your debut book. But there's little point in expending energy on an email list or paying to build an author website if you don't have a book to market yet. That's why unpublished writers should spend the bulk of their time and energy finishing their debut books, only giving serious thought to platform development and prelaunch marketing strategies in the months leading up to an established launch date. Debut authors who feel overwhelmed by the self-publishing process can skip the stress of platform development altogether in favor of simply getting their books out there. Remember that you're in this for the long haul. It's OK to take it one step at a time when you're getting started. You can always establish your platform, market your books, and expand your reach *after* you've published your debut book.

Regardless, many unpublished authors enjoy sharing their writing progress on dedicated social media accounts, and doing so can be a great way to make early connections with writers and readers. If this idea appeals to you, go ahead and create your social media presence. You can use the "build in public" strategy we'll discuss in chapter 19 to generate early visibility for your book.

Understanding Author Branding

As you build your platform, remember to brand your work. In marketing terms, **branding** refers to the process of developing the features that distinguish one company or product from another. Your author brand is what makes your creative work unique. It's how readers will describe your books—and, by extension, the entirety of your platform—based on how you present your work to the world.

In defining your creative niche during chapter 5, you've already struck at the heart of your author brand. You've identified what you write, who you write for, and how those elements differentiate your work from other authors' books and stories. Centering this niche as you build each cornerstone of your platform is key.

One of the ways you can ensure that your readers understand your brand is to develop consistent visual and copy-based branding that highlights your creative niche. If you write crime thrillers, your branding should consist of bold fonts, dark colors, and emotionally resonant copy that contains words like *heart-racing, bloodcurdling,* and *suspenseful.* And if you write children's craft books, you'll want to favor a bright color palette and whimsical copy instead. See how that works?

Each aspect of your author brand should work in tandem to give readers an immediate impression of your creative niche. If readers who land on your website or view your book listings can't determine whether you write sweet or steamy romance, you might have an issue on your hands. The same principle applies to historical versus contemporary fiction, business versus personal finance books, and so on.

To avoid confusing readers, take some time to define the parameters of your brand. What kind of language will (and won't) you use across your platform? What colors, fonts, and imagery will attract your ideal audience? How do you want readers to feel after reading one of your books or newsletters? What steps will you take to consistently manifest this atmosphere in your work? Make your ideal readers feel at home across all aspects of your platform, and you'll soon develop a devoted readership who can't wait to follow each step of your publishing journey.

16

CONTENT MARKETING: BLOGS, PODCASTS, AND VIDEO

C ontent marketing is a type of pull marketing in which a writer builds a secondary body of work designed to attract their ideal reader. This body of work acts as a platform, helping the writer gain the visibility and credibility they need to sell their published books.

Not sure what content marketing looks like? Think of the poet who runs a thriving Instagram poetry account, the personal finance guru who promotes their books through their YouTube channel, or the memoirist who publishes personal essays on Medium. Content marketing is most beneficial for nonfiction authors who need the visibility and credibility of an established audience to sell books. However, fiction authors can also take advantage of content marketing to boost their reach and revenue. Consider the horror novelist who shares creepy short stories on their podcast or the historical romance author who posts interesting research fun facts on their blog.

Whatever its iteration, content marketing is most effective at extending an author's reach and selling power when the body of work they create provides free valuable insights or entertainment. For example, I've built a thriving audience through my work at Well-Storied by publishing hundreds of articles on writing, publishing, and creative living. These articles attract readers who are likely to enjoy my books, workbooks, and workshops. By giving generously without demanding a dime, I've built an audience who values the content I create—and who, in turn, are eager to purchase my paid resources as well. However, before you decide to follow in my footsteps, first consider whether content marketing is an expense you're willing to incur.

The High Cost of Content Marketing

Monetarily speaking, most forms of content marketing are free to employ beyond initial setup costs (e.g., a microphone for podcasting, a camera for YouTube videography). But time is money, and building and maintaining a secondary body of work takes a *lot* of time. That's why high-volume authors rarely engage in content marketing. They simply don't have the time to develop a blog or YouTube channel when they're cranking out three or more books a year—at least not without the aid of one or more paid team members. Instead, you'll typically find high-volume authors running intense paid advertising campaigns, which can help them reach thousands of readers without the same intensive time commitment.

With that in mind, you might be wondering why any author would invest their time in content marketing when they could simply publish books at a faster pace. It's a good question and one that's worth exploring.

As I previously mentioned, content marketing is essential for expository nonfiction authors who need credibility to sell books. In my case, by generously offering free value to my readers at Well-Storied, I've proven the value that my books and paid resources hold. Without that credibility, it's unlikely that I could successfully sell books about the writing life.

Readers simply wouldn't have reason to trust in my expertise on the topic.

Beyond the need for credibility, many authors simply can't publish multiple books a year. Some authors write in research-intensive genres. Others experience chronic pain or mental illness that makes consistent writing difficult. Never mind the daily responsibilities such as day jobs, young children, and ailing parents that can eat away at the time and energy one needs for writing. In all of these cases, content marketing can be a great way for authors to maintain relationships with their readers between book launches.

Content marketing can also be a great way for authors who publish in less popular niches to develop their readerships. A literary novelist, for example, may find it difficult to sell a significant number of books through paid advertising. The unfortunate truth is that most readers exclusively consume genre fiction. However, the same literary novelist may have more luck developing an engaged readership by creating a blog or YouTube channel dedicated to teaching and reviewing literary fiction. The free, easy-to-consume content would attract their ideal readers. The author could then start each post or video with a quick introduction to promote their published books to their audience.

Many authors worry that content marketing will steal valuable time and energy from their book-related work. This is a valid concern, especially for those who don't have much time or energy to devote to their creative pursuits in the first place. However, content marketing rarely requires the same *type* of energy as writing a book. Consider the difference between revising an epic fantasy novel and running a worldbuilding podcast or drafting a book of knitting patterns and teaching the basics of the craft on Instagram. For many authors, content marketing can help maximize—rather than limit—their daily creative potential, ultimately enabling them to balance writing and marketing with ease.

For some authors, content marketing can simplify the process of writing their books and vice versa. For example, I first wrote about some of the topics in *Self-Publishing Simplified* on my blog. When it came time to outline the book, I pulled relevant content from my blog archives and reworked it into book format. Similarly, when I published *Build Your Best Writing Life*, I shared multiple excerpts from the book on my blog as a form of content marketing.

Finally, content marketing can help authors create alternative streams of income. Authors can host ads, create sponsored content, and post affiliate links to products their audience may enjoy. They can also create other paid products such as video courses and workbooks that are related to their creative work.

All in all, there's no denying that content marketing takes time. Building a successful secondary body of work can take just as long as developing a sizable backlist. That's why it's important to only pursue content marketing if you're genuinely passionate about your **medium** (i.e., the topics you plan to cover as well as the platform where you'll build your body of work). Passion doesn't mean the work will always be easy, especially in the early days when you haven't yet developed your skills on your platform of choice. But if you're energized by the idea of running a podcast, starting a YouTube channel, or blogging to attract an engaged readership, content marketing is an avenue worth exploring.

Key Tips for Successful Content Marketing

If you're interested in giving content marketing a try, first take a moment to learn how to effectively build your body of work.

Tip 1: (Re)Define Your Creative Niche

First things first—niche down. Remember that you aren't trying to attract every reader on the planet. Rather, you're trying to attract your *ideal* reader. You'll find it much easier to build your audience and sell more books if you focus on creating content exclusively for the readers who are most likely to love your books. And the more specific, the better.

All the same, don't assume that your content needs to be entirely unique. There are thousands of writing blogs on the internet, and mine was far from the first. The reason why I've found success with Well-Storied is that my approach to the craft differs subtly from many other approaches. I'm concerned with helping writers overcome the internal roadblocks that stand in the way of their best writing lives, which is a niche topic in the online writing world. I still cover storytelling principles and publishing advice, but I always focus on creating content that's actionable *and* encouraging. That's my style. It might not be every writer's cup of tea, but it's the right brew for the writers I want to reach.

I've also niched down at Well-Storied by publishing content solely related to novels. I don't cover nonfiction, short fiction, or poetry beyond the occasional guest post from an author who produces those types of works. The only reason I've widened my lens with the book you're reading is because the process of publishing and marketing a book is largely the same for indie authors regardless of the nature of their work. It simply didn't make sense to alienate a large portion of writers by speaking solely to novelists on these topics.

When getting started with content marketing, it's OK if you don't yet know your **hook** (i.e., what makes your work unique). I went through several phases in my writing at Well-Storied before getting to the heart of my voice. However, it's a good idea to niche down as early as possible. Your content can always expand or evolve over time. However, by being specific from the start, you'll expedite the process of reaching new readers while building your secondary platform from the ground up.

Tip 2: Go Big or Go Home

Here's a tip that may surprise you: when getting started with content marketing, it's better to create *quantity* rather than *quality*. Some indie authors think that producing high-quality work is the quickest way to attract an audience in saturated online circles. However, building a successful content marketing platform is a long-term endeavor that requires both passion and skill.

On the passion front, it's difficult to know whether the energy you have for a new-to-you project will prove enduring until you start putting in the work. In my early days of creative entrepreneurship, I thought I wanted to run a book-related YouTube channel alongside my work at Well-Storied. Excited, I dove in, creating dozens of videos over several months before realizing that I loathed—absolutely *loathed*—video editing. It just wasn't for me. So I tried a new avenue instead, creating audio editions of my Well-Storied articles to share via podcast. Audio editing proved to be much less painful, and I ran *The Well-Storied Podcast* with great success for years. (In January 2022, I began hosting a new podcast called *Joyful Writing*.) By pursuing quantity over quality with my YouTube channel, I determined that this platform wasn't right for me much more quickly than I would have if I'd only published a handful of high-quality videos within the same time frame.

Also, most content marketing platforms require unique skills. No one is born with an innate understanding of how to work the Instagram algorithm or tweak website design with basic code. If you try to create effective and enticing content from day one, you'll never finish a thing. Your sky-high standards will ground your content marketing efforts before they ever reach deep water. So be willing to produce "bad" content. Each piece of OK work will teach you how to level up your content creation skills—and you may just discover your unique voice in the process. A win-win scenario for you, right?

Tip 3: Develop a Content Creation System

Most forms of content marketing require frequent and consistent new content. If you don't have a plan in place for cultivating and executing new content ideas, you'll struggle to maintain the platform you're trying to build.

Before kick-starting your content marketing efforts, take an afternoon to brainstorm as many content ideas as you can. As a general rule of thumb, if you have trouble generating a year's worth of ideas within your niche without turning to the internet for help, you might not be knowledgeable enough (yet!) to build and maintain your platform. Consider repeating this process every few months to ensure that you can sustain your content marketing efforts. For example, even though I'm over seven years into blogging, I can think of hundreds of niche-related topics I can still cover. If you struggle with this, it isn't necessarily time to call it quits or decide not to get started in the first place. Rather, it's time to make learning an active part of your writing life.

One of the reasons why I have so many ideas for new articles, books, and other projects is that I've made a habit of consuming content related to my creative work. Books, blogs, YouTube videos, educational social media accounts—I devour them all by taking a few small bites each day. To maximize recall, I take notes in my **second brain** (a term coined by productivity expert Tiago Forte), a digital system for storing ideas and information. To learn more about this concept, check out the Well-Storied article titled "How Writers Can Organize

Creative Work in a Second Brain," which is available at https://www.well-storied.com/writingpractice.

Active learning might sound like another time-consuming activity to add to your busy schedule, but it's essential to your growth as a writer and a marketer. Remember that learning begets growth. No artist ever evolved by remaining stagnant in their understanding of their craft—and you won't either. The good news is that active learning doesn't have to require a huge daily commitment. For instance, you can read an article during your lunch break, listen to a podcast during your commute, or take ten minutes before bed to watch a YouTube video from your favorite content creator. Most of us spend far too much time mindlessly consuming low-value content as it is. You have the power to change that. Start small.

That being said, curating new ideas is only half of a good content creation system. The other half requires you to execute on your ideas, transforming them into content that will increase your reach and revenue. Different productivity techniques work well for different authors. Some benefit most from batching their work, blocking out time to create as much content as possible. Others excel by creating content in the margins of their lives, putting in a few focused minutes of work whenever they have time to spare. All progress is good progress. The most important thing is that you figure out which process works best for you.

Tip 4: Invite Community

The point of content marketing is to attract and engage an audience of ideal readers. Don't neglect the latter half of this mission by failing to give readers a way to engage with your content. Build community through comments, easy-to-share links, and direct lines of contact. Give your audience a way to interact with one another if possible. Most importantly, make sure that *you* interact with *them*. Readers remember and support authors who make them feel seen, and authors can find a greater sense of joy and fulfillment in marketing by engaging with their biggest fans.

Tip 5: Remember to Level Up

While quality doesn't matter greatly when you first begin content marketing, it will certainly impact your long-term success. Once you've determined that a platform is right for you, work on actively improving the quality of the content you produce. You don't need to go from 0 to 100 on the production front. Instead, acknowledge how you can improve your work, then take tiny actions to manifest that improvement. For instance, you could learn how to enhance the lighting in your YouTube videos, purchase a better microphone for your podcast, or identify all the filler words you frequently use in your blog posts and then cull them from your work.

At no point do you need to produce the best content ever created. There will always be someone who's doing things "better" than you—someone with more time, money, experience, or support. That's OK. Creating content isn't a competition. It's a marketing strategy. As long as you're attracting an audience of readers who love your books, you're doing just fine. Improving your content is simply the best way to continue extending your reach and revenue, and if you're passionate about your content, there's a good chance you'll find joy in the challenge as well.

Tip 6: Get Social

Engaging with your audience through your secondary body of work is a great way to build strong relationships with your readers. However, connecting with fellow content creators is the best way to maximize the visibility of your platform.

Consider writing guest posts, booking podcast interviews, or collaborating with fellow YouTubers in your niche. You could also cohost an Instagram Live event or run a webinar with a creator you adore. The choice is up to you!

Note that you don't have to participate in these types of collaborations often to benefit from them. A few high-value partnerships per year can rapidly broaden your audience. It's also common for such collaborations to lead to ongoing working relationships and friendships. Talk about another win-win!

Tip 7: Remember to Promote Your Work

Building a notable secondary body of work requires a major investment of time and energy. To make the most of this investment, remember why you created your platform in the first place: to promote your books!

Many authors hesitate to pitch their books online. They worry that their newfound audience will desert them the second they promote a paid product. Unfortunately, this fear will ring true for some members of your audience. Every time I host a sale or promote an affiliate product I love, I get an email from someone telling me that I'm greedy for "pushing" them to buy something. That's just how some people are, and their words and actions are no reflection on you as an author or a content creator. Let those people go. They weren't your ideal readers anyway.

By not promoting your published books, you're hurting both yourself and the ideal reader who would love to get their hands on your book. Remember that good marketing always serves the reader. You thrive when they thrive. So go ahead and pitch your work, put a link in your profile, mention your book at the beginning of a video or the end of a podcast episode, or include a direct pitch in each new blog post you write. Whatever the case may be, if you don't pitch your book, you'll never transform your new audience into a dedicated readership.

So make your content marketing efforts worthwhile. Pitch your book loudly and proudly, and watch your readership grow.

17

EMAIL MARKETING: NEWSLETTERS, INCENTIVES, AND SALES FUNNELS

Earlier in part 3, you learned how an email list is one of the most powerful and versatile tools in an author's book marketing arsenal. You also discovered how an email list provides authors with a direct line of contact to their biggest fans and how to establish your email list. In this chapter, it's time to explore basic email marketing strategies as well as ways to get readers on your email list in the first place. Let's start with the former.

Generally speaking, authors can leverage their email lists to benefit their marketing efforts and the strength of their readership in eight ways:

1. Pitch their books in emails sent to their lists. This tactic is most effective during launches and limited-time price drops (i.e., seasonal sales).
2. Use their email lists to build what's known as an advance reader team, a small subset of subscribers who receive ARCs of an author's books from the author in exchange for ratings, reviews, and hype.
3. Source beta readers from among their email lists,

allowing interested fans to take part in the creation of their upcoming books.

4. Network with fellow writers and creatives by cross-promoting their work via email.

5. Send emails to their list to promote their latest free content, such as a blog post, YouTube video, or podcast episode.

6. Target paid ads to reach their email subscribers by loading a list of subscriber email addresses into advertising networks such as Facebook Ads.

7. Generate alternative income streams by participating in affiliate opportunities or selling related products (e.g., online courses, digital workbooks) that they promote via their email list.

8. Strengthen their relationships with readers by sending personalized newsletters that contain exclusive, high-value content.

Nonfiction authors with content marketing platforms often make use of most or all of these email marketing strategies, sending frequent emails to maximize their income through teaching, coaching, or consulting. On the other hand, fiction authors often use fewer email marketing strategies and favor exclusive behind-the-scenes content rather than prescriptive or informational emails.

Consistency may be key to effective email marketing, but consistency doesn't need to mean high frequency. Many fiction authors only send one email a month. However, it's important to establish what readers can expect from your email list and regularly meet those expectations. This rule applies to everything you create as an author: your books, your content, and your social media posts. When you meet readers' expectations for your work, you maintain their interest and attention. When you fail to meet their expectations, you risk losing their valuable readership. Expectations are a form of trust, a pact between author and readers that ensures a strong relationship. This doesn't mean you can't expand or shift readers' expectations for your work over time, but it does mean that you must take care to avoid disrupting all the time and effort you've put into building your readership in the first place.

What Should You Send to Your Email List?

In breaking down the eight ways authors use their email lists as book marketing tools, I've given you a few ideas for the types of content you can send to your subscribers. But you won't always have a new book to launch, beta readers to seek, or a new digital product to pitch. In between those moments, you can use your email list to strengthen and maintain your relationship with readers. What are some examples of exclusive, high-value content you can send via email to connect with your subscribers? You have more options than you might expect.

Readers across all fiction genres love a peek behind the curtain, so to speak. If you write fiction, consider sharing an aspect of your writing process (e.g., the environment in which you work best, what your story development process looks like), an update on your work in progress, or an excerpt from an upcoming book. You could also share an in-depth look at one of your characters, a fun fact about your story world, or an interesting research factoid. And how about a bonus chapter or scene cut from one of your published books? Other ideas include the inspiration behind your latest novel, an explanation of what drew you to the genre you write, or a story about how you relate to one of your books' characters.

If you write expository nonfiction, your readers may expect to receive lessons or information related to your field of choice. As long as you know your field well enough to write multiple books on its subject matter, brainstorming ideas for expository emails shouldn't be too difficult. Be of service, and readers will find value in the emails you send.

If you write narrative nonfiction or poetry, you'll need to take a different approach. Consider sharing exclusive stories or poems that aren't found in your published works. You could also share a list of your favorite memoirists or poets, notes concerning the inspirations behind your creative work, or conversations about the personal importance of the most prevalent themes in your books. A good ol' peek at your creative process is never a bad idea either.

There are also different types of content that authors can include in their emails regardless of the nature of their work. Exclusive book cover reveals, notes celebrating writing milestones, and links to interviews or media mentions are always good ideas. You can also include readers in your creation process whenever possible. For example, you could ask readers to share feedback on potential book titles or allow them to name a character in your next book. Finally, you can always invite readers to engage with you by hosting a Q&A.

Still unsure of what to write in your emails? Consider what you'd like to ask your favorite author if you met them face-to-face at an event. Do you have any questions about their work? Are you curious about their writing or research process, their educational background, or what they're working on next? Consider watching a few author interview videos on YouTube to get an idea of what readers like to know. Finally, remember that you can glean email content ideas by subscribing to the lists of authors who write comparable books to yours.

How Can You Encourage Readers to Subscribe to Your List?

Knowing what to send to your email list is one thing. Building a list of readers who you can email is another thing altogether. In chapter 15, I discussed how to establish your email list and give readers opportunities to subscribe via your website, social media accounts, and backlist. But how can you actually encourage readers to subscribe to your list?

Telling readers about all the cool, exclusive content you'll send them can be enticing. However, most people don't want to receive more emails. They already have enough content to consume, and most aren't looking for more. That's why you need to give them an extra reason to sign up for your list—an incentive, so to speak.

In the email marketing world, an incentive is a valuable piece of bonus material that readers receive for free when they sign up for your list. It acts as both a form of encouragement and a show of gratitude because for authors and other marketers, an email address is one of their businesses' most valuable assets. It's the key that unlocks a direct line of contact to their customer base. To respect the value of this asset, and to effectively encourage readers to sign up for your list, the incentive you offer should always be free and exclusive to your subscribers. It should also closely mirror the nature of the books you publish. But what does this incentive look like?

If you write fiction, high-value incentives include short stories, novellas, and full-length books. You could even offer a bonus prologue, epilogue, or deleted scene. Expository nonfiction authors might also offer a short or full-length book, or they might pitch a digital guide, free video workshop, or email course. And if you write narrative nonfiction or poetry, your incentive might be a free short story, journaling guide, or poetry collection. As with email content ideas, the easiest way to brainstorm the types of incentives you offer readers is to see what similar authors are doing.

Many established authors offer multiple incentives to readers who sign up for their lists. For example, indie thriller author Mark Dawson offers what he calls the Mark Dawson Starter Library, a collection of exclusive short stories and novellas related to his various book series. Generally speaking, the higher the value of your bonus material, the more likely it will encourage readers to sign up for your list. However, don't feel pressured to offer multiple incentives (or even a single full-length book) if you're at the beginning of your publishing journey. The most important thing you can do as a debut author is write your second book. When it comes to your email list, a small offering will still entice the right readers to sign up for your list.

If you're a debut author who's short on time, you might not want to create a distinct short offering to serve as an incentive. That's OK. You're in this for the long haul, and you have plenty of time to beef up your sign-up bonus as your writing career progresses. For now, consider offering a sneak peek at your second book. This could be an early draft of the opening chapters or simply a detailed book description that readers can't find elsewhere on the internet. Anything related to your work will do when you're first getting your feet—or rather your writing career—off the ground.

Understanding Email Marketing Funnels

By implementing an incentive to encourage readers to sign up for your list, you've created the second stage of your email marketing funnel.

In marketing terms, a **funnel** is a system for transforming leads into paying customers. For authors, this means a system of turning potential readers into longtime members of your readership. The great thing about marketing funnels is that they're a largely passive way of marketing your book. In most cases, you only need to create content for your funnel once, then set up your system. Readers can then journey through your funnel at any time, consuming content designed to encourage them to purchase one or more of your books.

Most email marketing funnels contain four stages:

1. Awareness
2. Incentive
3. Engagement
4. Payment

The first stage of your funnel, Awareness, introduces readers to the knowledge that your email list exists. You can passively increase the visibility of your email list by including links and sign-up forms on your website and social media accounts, as well as in the back matter of your published books. You can also *actively* encourage awareness of your email list through visibility marketing techniques such as writing guest blog posts or participating in podcast interviews where you can mention your email list and its incentive.

The second stage of your email marketing funnel is Incentive. This is the point at which readers sign up for your list to access your incentive. Make sure that this process is as simple as possible. Readers shouldn't have to jump through hoops to get their hands on your incentive. Instead, offer an easy download link as soon as possible. Some authors do so in an automated welcome email, while others redirect readers to a landing page on their website with a download link after readers have subscribed. The choice is up to you.

If you're offering a digital book, short story, or novella as your incentive, consider using BookFunnel, an author service that specializes in delivering e-books and audiobooks to readers when purchased or gifted directly. BookFunnel handles the technical and customer service ends of digital book delivery, meaning that you never have to walk a reader through the process of sending an e-book file to their Kindle or otherwise accessing your resources. You can also use BookFunnel to send ARCs to readers and sell box sets, among other features.

Engagement, the third stage in your email marketing funnel, is where you connect with readers through ongoing emails using all of the ideas I mentioned earlier in this chapter. As you engage with your readers, you'll have opportunities to pitch and promote your books. If a reader chooses to purchase them, they'll travel down to the fourth and final stage of your funnel, which is Payment. Congratulations, writer! You've now turned a potential reader into a paying customer and, with any luck, a longtime member of your readership. Now you can continue engaging with that reader, offering them consistent and exclusive high-value content while occasionally promoting your existing books and new releases.

Harnessing the Power of a Welcome Sequence

Before we wrap up this chapter on email marketing, let's revisit the Engagement stage of your new email marketing funnel.

Engaging your email list on an ongoing basis by sending consistent, high-value emails is a great way to nurture the relationship you've built with your existing subscribers. But what about the readers who've just signed up for your email list? Let's say that you only send one email a month. If a new subscriber signs up for your list the day after you send an email, they won't hear from you again for another thirty days. By that time, they might not remember who you are—or, because you haven't yet established what they can expect as your email subscriber, they might think you don't care enough to consistently get in touch. Ouch. Not a great first impression, right?

To avoid these pitfalls and misconceptions, consider creating an automated welcome sequence that new subscribers will receive starting the day they subscribe to your list. Ideally, this welcome sequence will be short and sweet. You don't want to inundate your new subscribers with lengthy emails several days in a row. However, you do want to explain to subscribers who you are, what you write, and what they can expect now that they've signed up for your list. Here's an example of what such a sequence might look like:

> **Email 1:** Welcome the subscriber to your list. Briefly introduce yourself, tell them what you write, and offer a download link for the incentive you promised. Be sure to use language that aligns with your creative niche.
>
> **Email 2:** Tell a short, engaging story about what led you to write within your creative niche that ultimately introduces subscribers to your debut novel or the first book in your series. Encourage subscribers to purchase the book by linking to common marketplaces. Some subscribers will have already read your book, so kindly ask those readers to leave a quick rating and review. Remind them to use the links you've included to easily reach your book's listing pages.
>
> **Email 3:** Give subscribers a sneak peek at your work in progress and encourage them to follow your writing journey through the emails you plan to send. Establish what they can expect from your emails, and remind them that they can download your incentive or purchase your books at any time. Again, provide easy download and book listing links.

As you publish more books, you can add new emails to your welcome sequence that introduce subscribers to these books. Or you may want to keep your welcome sequence short and sweet and rely on your nonautomated emails for additional book marketing. There's no right or wrong approach here, and the best way to structure your welcome sequence will always be the way that helps you effectively engage with new subscribers. So don't be afraid to play around with your sequence and add new content over time. A willingness to tinker and test is what helps indie authors find and maintain financial success as the industry evolves.

As for the technical aspects of implementing a welcome sequence, every major email marketing service has an automation feature, and most of them include this feature in their base pricing package (or for free!). The great thing about automation, of course, is that it's a completely passive way to engage your subscribers. That statement might sound devoid of heart, but it doesn't have to be. You're one person—an author who will, with any luck, soon have dozens (if not hundreds or thousands) of new subscribers joining your list. Engaging with each subscriber personally and promptly is impossible. But you can write a great welcome sequence full of heart that will automatically find its way into each new subscriber's inbox, ensuring that you make a positive first impression that keeps them coming back for more.

If a new subscriber doesn't purchase one of your books after reading your welcome sequence, that's OK. Some readers will eagerly gobble up everything you offer, while others will need more time to commit. The great thing is that you now have a direct line of contact with those readers, which will allow you to send high-value content that proves why your books will be their next great reads.

18

PAID ADVERTISING: AMAZON, FACEBOOK, AND BOOKBUB

P aid advertising is what it says on the tin. Authors pay to advertise their books to a specific audience on popular online book marketplaces, social media platforms, and book promotion sites. They can also use paid advertising on social media to promote other entities related to their platforms, such as the free incentive they offer to their email list subscribers or their latest blog post.

Many new authors find paid advertising more intimidating than other book marketing efforts, both from technical and monetary standpoints. There's certainly a steep learning curve to creating your first ad campaign, no matter which network you're using. It's also much easier for some authors to spend money on website setup or recording equipment than on ad campaigns that report whether you've broken even. The fear of failure keeps many authors from exploring paid advertising opportunities, which is a shame given the many ways authors can leverage ads to grow their platforms and market their books.

Specifically, five types of authors can benefit from running paid book ads:

1. Authors who have a decent marketing budget and want to maximize the reach of their books
2. High-volume authors who want to maximize the number of books they can write by avoiding more time-consuming marketing strategies
3. Debut authors who have little to no platform and want to get their books in front of their ideal readers as soon as possible
4. Authors who want to promote a limited-time price drop to spike their book sales
5. Authors who want to use ads in combination with other marketing strategies to spike their sales so they can hit traditional best-seller lists

If you fall into one of these categories, consider giving paid advertising a try. There may be a learning curve to creating paid advertising campaigns, but the same could be said for any other marketing technique. Plus, you don't need to throw hundreds of dollars at paid advertising from the start. Most networks allow you to cap your daily **ad spend** (i.e., the amount of money needed to run an online paid advertisement) or the total cost of your ad campaign, so you never need to worry that you'll wake up one day to find that an ad has drained your bank account dry.

However, before creating an ad on most platforms, you'll need to ensure that your book has a great title, cover design, and description. While you can run nearly any book ad you please on sites like Amazon and Facebook, most book promotion sites will refuse to run an ad if the book's quality doesn't match their professional standards. Those same sites are also known to reject ads for books that don't have great ratings or reviews, and many will only promote books that fall into popular fiction and nonfiction genres. If you're a debut author, consider sticking to Amazon Ads and Facebook Ads until your book has garnered enough traction there. These two ad networks also work best for established indie authors who write in less commercial markets.

An Introduction to Amazon Ads

If you've listed a book for sale through Amazon KDP, you can use the Amazon Ads network to run paid book advertising campaigns. Currently, you can run three types of campaigns through this network: Sponsored Products ads, Sponsored Brands ads, and Lockscreen ads.

Sponsored Products ads appear on relevant search result pages in your Amazon marketplace of choice, as well as on individual product listings. If you've ever seen the "Products related to this item" section on an Amazon book listing, you've seen Sponsored Products ads at work. The only downside to Sponsored Product ads is that you can only promote one book at a time. If you'd like to run an ad promoting up to three books at once, then you'll want to run a Sponsored Brands ad campaign. These ads display in various spots within your Amazon marketplace of choice, most noticeably at the top of relevant search results pages, and can be a great way to promote a book series. The final type of campaign you can run, Lockscreen ads, causes your ad to appear on readers' Kindle lock screens. With Lockscreen ads, you can typically promote just one book at a time.

When creating any of these ad campaigns, you'll need to enter a list of relevant keywords that the algorithm will use to determine which shoppers see your ad. Effective keywords are words or phrases that your ideal readers might plug into the Amazon search bar when looking for their next great read. So if you've written a sword-and-sorcery fantasy novel, your campaign's keywords might include the following:

- Epic fantasy
- Magical quest
- Brandon Sanderson
- Lord of the Rings
- Chosen one fantasy

Relevant keywords boost the number of **impressions** your ad receives, which is the number of times your ad is shown to Amazon shoppers. When monitoring your ad campaign, you'll also see data on how many shoppers click through your ad to view your book's listing, as well as how many orders (i.e., sales) your ad has generated. From these three data points—impressions, clicks, and orders—Amazon Ads derives two metrics that determine the overall success of your ad campaign.

Metric 1: Click-Through Rate (CTR)

This is your ad's ratio of clicks to impressions. In essence, CTR indicates the percentage of shoppers who clicked on your ad to learn more about your book. The higher your ad's CTR, the better.

Metric 2: Advertising Cost of Sale (ACoS)

Your ad's ACoS is the percentage of its generated sales revenue that you spent running the ad. ACoS is calculated by dividing your sales revenue by your ad spend. The lower your ACoS, the more effective your ad campaign.

With Amazon Ads, your campaign's ad spend is determined by the number of clicks your ad receives rather than sales or impressions. If your ad receives a large number of impressions but no clicks, you won't spend a dime. But if your ad receives a large number of clicks but no sales, you'll be in the red. Therefore, it's important to ensure that your ad copy, book title, and cover design accurately represent your book and that your book's listing—especially its description and available sample—effectively entices readers to purchase a copy.

Note that most of your initial ad campaigns won't return huge profits. It takes time to build **relevance**—the metric by which Amazon determines how many shoppers see your ad—within the Amazon Ads algorithm. The greater your relevance, the more impressions your campaigns will receive, thus allowing you to scale your ads to make more significant income. To build relevance, you need to prove to Amazon that your ads can generate a high CTR and a low ACoS. In other words, if Amazon sees that a high percentage of shoppers not only click on your ads but purchase the product you're promoting, it will increase the pool of shoppers who see your campaigns. The greater your ad's reach, the more revenue it's likely to return.

Consider treating your first six months with Amazon Ads as a learning experience. Review your campaign statistics frequently to identify which keywords result in clicks and sales. Create multiple campaigns to test different sets of keywords and sales copy, and see what sticks. If your ads aren't performing well despite strong keywords and ad copy, consider revamping your book's title, cover design, or description. Study the data and continue honing your ad campaigns, and you'll soon develop powerful relevance within the Amazon Ads network that will allow you to grow your readership and skyrocket your sales.

An Introduction to Facebook Ads

In recent years, the Facebook Ads network has become a highly valuable tool in authors' book marketing tool belts. Its robust campaign features make it easy to target a wide variety of readers and achieve a wide variety of objectives like the following:

- Promoting a book launch or limited-time price drop
- Boosting the reach of a preferred post on your Facebook author page, such as a book launch announcement or popular blog post
- Building your email list through lead generation or conversion ads
- Increasing event responses for your virtual book launch party or webinar
- Increasing traffic to your Facebook author page or website

Facebook Ads can feature images, image carousels, videos, or product collections. You can also select where your ad will appear in Facebook's interface. Options include a user's feed, the right-hand side of Facebook's desktop interface, and Facebook Stories. Additionally, you can use the Facebook Ads network to run paid ads on Instagram since both apps are under the same corporate ownership. However, you'll need an Instagram business account to run ads on Instagram.

After deciding what your ad will feature and where it will appear, you can target your ad to reach a specific set of users. This set can include your email list subscribers (simply import their addresses when creating your campaign audience), people who like and interact with your Facebook author page, and people who like and interact with content related to relevant keywords. You can also tailor your audience according to age, gender, and location, or you can target users who follow other authors' fan pages, among other options. No matter the audience you target for your campaign, always ensure that they fall within the sphere of your ideal readership. There's little point in targeting users who follow Stephen King's fan page if you write contemporary romance, for example. Keep your creative niche in mind as you build your ads, and your paid marketing efforts will always pay off.

Speaking of finances, it's important to note that Facebook Ads can be very cheap to run. You can build your first campaigns for as little as a few bucks a day. However, of all the paid advertising opportunities, Facebook Ads has the steepest learning curve thanks to its complex range of options. The sheer scope of the network's features makes a useful introduction difficult to package into an overview as I did with Amazon Ads. However, with Facebook boasting nearly three billion users worldwide, there's a good chance that most of your ideal readers spend at least a small portion of their week on the site. So taking the time to learn how to use Facebook Ads will be worth your effort.

If you're eager to get started with Facebook Ads, then check out Mark Dawson's "Ads for Authors," a popular online course that details the process of running successful paid ad campaigns on Facebook, Amazon, and BookBub. You can learn more about the course at https://www.selfpublishingformula.com/courses. Alternatively, if you're looking for a great free resource that offers a detailed look at how authors can use Facebook Ads, then review the Kindlepreneur article titled "How to Advertise a Book on Facebook," which you can find at https://www.kindlepreneur.com/facebook-ads-for-books.

An Introduction to Book Promotion Sites

Book promotion sites are free services for readers that compile current digital book discounts across the web. These sites frequently send email blasts to subscribed readers that contain an overview of the weekly discounts available in their chosen genres. Many of these sites also offer indie authors the opportunity to purchase paid ads that promote their limited-time price drops.

Among the various book promotion sites available to readers, BookBub is by far the most popular one with over ten million subscribers from around the world. As an author, you can run four types of promotions with BookBub.

Type 1: BookBub Ads

This is BookBub's self-serve advertising platform, which you can use to run ads for books in any format and at any point in a book's life cycle. You can promote a preorder campaign, new release, or discount, or you can simply boost the visibility of a full-priced book. You can also promote books of any length, as well as single-author and multiauthor box sets. BookBub Ads is also the most flexible of BookBub's advertising options. You can use this platform to target many types of audiences at various price points. Purchased BookBub Ads then appear in dedicated spaces on the BookBub site and within their email blasts.

Type 2: Featured Deals

This type of BookBub promotion features the best limited-time book deals using email blasts that are sent to millions of readers around the world. To maintain the integrity of these deals, BookBub's editorial team curates these ads specifically for their highly engaged audience, meaning that authors must submit their Featured Deals for approval. Featured Deals are often more expensive to run than BookBub Ads, but they frequently result in significant sales spikes and increased visibility. Authors can use Featured Deals to promote books of any length or format as well as box sets. However, only perma-free (i.e., permanently free) books and books discounted by at least 50 percent are eligible.

Type 3: New Releases for Less

Similar to Featured Deals, this type of promotion is curated by BookBub's editorial team. However, New Releases for Less solely features the best in new low-priced e-book releases. E-books don't need to be discounted to meet eligibility requirements, but they do need to be listed for $6 or less, and only full-length books are eligible. As with Featured Deals, authors must submit this type of promotion for approval and can expect a higher price tag in exchange for the exclusive visibility.

Type 4: Chirp's Audiobook Deals

Chirp is an audiobook service powered by BookBub through which readers can purchase audiobooks without a subscription. Indie authors can distribute their audiobooks to Chirp through Findaway Voices, the audiobook distribution platform first mentioned in chapter 13. Authors can then use Chirp's "Audiobook Deals" page to promote limited-time pricing discounts to Chirp users. As with Featured Deals and New Releases for Less, Chirp audiobook deals are curated by Book-Bub's editorial team and must be submitted for approval.

To improve the chances that your book will be approved for promotion as a Chirp audiobook deal (or for BookBub's Featured Deals or New Releases for Less), ensure that it has a fantastic cover and title, a great listing description, and many high-value ratings and reviews. You'll also find greater success with BookBub's curated promotion opportunities if your book falls into a popular genre.

Tips for Success with Paid Advertising

As with book marketing in general, achieving notable success with paid advertising takes time. On platforms like Amazon

Ads, you'll need to run successful ads on a small scale to build enough relevance for the platform to share your ads on a larger scale, thus allowing you to earn more revenue. Other advertising networks allow you to scale your ads immediately. But no matter the platform(s) you employ, you'll need to exercise a good amount of patience and persistence to determine which ad types, target audiences, and advertising budgets help you maximize your profit and visibility while minimizing your expenses.

All in all, most authors will find the effort of mastering paid advertising to be worthwhile. Many authors successfully promote their books for free via content and email marketing strategies. However, it's important to remember that many customers need repeated exposure to a product before they'll make a purchase. Running paid ads can be a great way to get your books in front of existing readers via another outlet while expanding your book's reach to new readers who haven't yet discovered your work.

While I mentioned many tips for paid advertising success when discussing the three most popular book ad networks, let's review a few additional tips that will help you make the most of your advertising budget.

Tip 1: Be Specific about What You Want to Achieve

Before creating any paid advertising campaign, determine who you want to reach and why. Be as specific as possible. There's a big difference between a "sweet romance novel" and a "sweet, small-town romance featuring a single dad and a city-worn heroine."

The same principle applies to your mission with running your ad. It's one thing to want to boost your book sales. It's another thing entirely to run a limited-time discount on your health and wellness book to maximize sales and visibility during the first week of January, when your ideal reader is desperately looking for guidance on how to keep their New Year's resolution to lose weight without losing their mind.

Tip 2: Hone Your Ad Copy to Convert Sales

Copywriting (i.e., the act of writing text intended to sell a product or service) is both an art and a craft. Good copywriting is also the difference between a paid ad that bombs and a paid ad that sees your book sales skyrocket. Understanding your ad's audience and mission will help you determine the best possible language to use when crafting your ad copy. However, it's also a good idea to learn a few basic copywriting principles. Ray Edwards's *How to Write Copy That Sells* is an excellent place to start.

Tip 3: Create Eye-Catching Imagery

With some networks (namely Facebook Ads), you can promote imagery other than a simple book cover. When using these networks, ensure that your imagery is as high-quality as the cover itself. Personally, I enjoy using Canva to create my ad imagery for free. However, many cover design companies and freelancers offer book advertising packages, which you can typically bundle with other services for a discounted rate.

Tip 4: Review Your Ads Frequently

Most indie authors review their ongoing ad campaigns once or twice a week, while high-volume authors or authors running intense limited-time campaigns often review their ads daily to ensure maximum reach and sales. It's important to keep an eye on your ad campaigns for several reasons. First, it's common for ads to work well for only a limited time. The campaign that made a killing last month might not do the same this month, and an author's failure to shut down a declining campaign could result in significant unnecessary ad spend.

Also, review your ads frequently to learn which audiences and keywords lead to the most conversions. You can then use this data to create new, higher-converting ad campaigns that will help you bring in more revenue than previous iterations. This process of testing and tinkering with ongoing ad campaigns is key to building relevance within the Amazon Ads network and cultivating ad campaigns that are effective enough to scale for greater revenue across all relevant paid advertising platforms.

Finally, remember that paid advertising doesn't always result in a direct return on investment, and that's OK. You might "lose" money by advertising your email list to new ideal readers on Facebook. But with any luck, the campaign will capture dozens—or even hundreds—of new subscribers to whom you can pitch your books via email for years to come. Alternatively, you might only make a small profit on a campaign that promotes a discounted book. But if that book is the first in a page-turning series, the new readers you reach are likely to purchase additional installments in the future, making your ad campaigns more cost-effective over time. So don't be afraid to seize paid advertising opportunities, writer. There's incredible possibility—and profit—to be found in investing in this type of promotion.

19

VISIBILITY MARKETING: INTERVIEWS, SPEAKING GIGS, AND COLLABORATIONS

A great way to grow your platform and reach more readers is through visibility marketing, which includes activities that are designed to help you extend the reach and credibility of your platform via platforms that are *not* under your direct control. Most visibility marketing strategies are therefore collaborative. Typically, another creative has built a platform comparable to yours in some way, and both parties agree to participate in a mutually beneficial collaboration. For instance, a podcaster gets you as a guest to interview on their show, and you get an opportunity to share your books with a new audience. Or a book blogger gets a free copy of your book in exchange for an honest review that, with any luck, will introduce your book to a wealth of new readers. And so your reach expands.

Online collaborations are the primary way that creatives network in the internet age, and these opportunities comprise the bulk of indie authors' visibility marketing efforts. Like many other forms of book marketing, your visibility marketing efforts often compound in interesting ways. A simple collaboration might lead to an ongoing relationship with a creator that proves to be mutually beneficial for years to come. Additionally, that same collaboration might lead to new networking opportunities as other creatives discover your work. Never mind the new readers who learn about your book, join your email list, and leave great ratings and reviews on your book's listings. Because of all these potential benefits, it can be difficult to quantify the rewards of visibility marketing. But there's no denying that a little up-front effort can lead to incredible growth in your reach and revenue, as well as additional lucrative opportunities down the road.

With that in mind, let's look at some of the most common ways that indie authors collaborate with other creatives to promote their work.

Guest Posts, Interviews, and Podcast Appearances

One of the most common visibility marketing strategies is to appear as a guest on another creator's blog, podcast, or YouTube channel. As a guest, you can create a piece of content to share on the creator's platform, such as a blog post about your research process or a video detailing your best worldbuilding tips. Alternatively, the creator may want to interview you or have you join them on their platform to discuss a particular topic related to your work.

In any case, this form of visibility marketing can be a great way to network with other creatives and reach new readers without putting forth a lot of time and effort. Most opportunities in this vein only require a few hours of work, including the time it takes to promote the collaboration to your existing readership. Most of these collaboration opportunities are also evergreen, meaning that readers can discover the content for years to come as they consume a creator's backlog of blog posts, podcast episodes, or YouTube videos. If you're smart about the opportunities you pursue and accept, your few hours of effort can generate notable reach and revenue for far longer than just a few days.

As a bonus, participating in collaborations of this nature can result in high-quality **backlinks** to your website. Receiving strong backlinks (i.e., incoming hyperlinks from one website to another) is one of the key factors that improve a website's SEO, or **search engine optimization**. In layman's terms, visibility marketing can help your author website rise through search engine rankings, generating greater traffic and reach.

As you develop your author platform and readership, you might find that some content creators will reach out to you with collaboration opportunities. However, in most cases, you'll need to pitch to content creators if you'd like to appear as a guest on their platform. You'll also need to pitch to them if you'd like to engage in the other types of visibility marketing we'll discuss in this chapter. Check out the final section in particular for tips on politely inviting other authors and creators to collaborate with you.

Social Media Collaborations

Indie authors can collaborate with other creators via social media. For example, it's common for authors to partner on give-aways designed to cross-pollinate their audiences or appear together in live streams. Some authors even swap social media accounts for a day to introduce their work to new readers. These types of collaborations typically work best for authors who share similar ideal audiences and already have a working relationship.

Book Blog Reviews

Word-of-mouth book recommendations hold incredible power —and no recommendation encourages readers to buy your book more effectively than a favorable review from a book blogger.

If you're not familiar with the world of online book reviews, a **book blogger** is an online influencer who publicly reviews books on their platform of choice. As the name suggests, many book bloggers post reviews on a blog. You can also find similar influencers on YouTube (try searching "BookTube") and Instagram (look for the #bookstagram hashtag). Other influencers build their audiences in Facebook reading groups or on Goodreads, the popular Amazon-owned book review site.

The online book review community is far-reaching, with many influencers earning full-time livings for their work. Many lesser-known influencers also run their platforms as hobbies or side hustles. Regardless of the size of their audience, book bloggers review books they receive for free in exchange for their honest, public opinion. Many of the most popular book bloggers partner exclusively with big-name traditional publishers. However, many book bloggers with notable followings also accept pitches from indie authors. Some even exclusively review self-published books.

Garnering a review from a popular book blogger is a great way to get more eyes on your books. It's also the only visibility marketing tactic where someone else creates content and pitches your book on your behalf. All you have to do is gift the reviewer a copy of your book in their preferred format. But don't make the mistake of sending your book to any book blogger who catches your eye. Most book bloggers don't accept unsolicited books. Instead, you'll need to pitch your book to the reviewer to see if they're interested in collaborating with you.

While you can pitch to book bloggers at any point in your book's life cycle, most indie authors seek reviews as a book launch marketing strategy. Some even put together a book blog tour, where multiple book bloggers post reviews of their book within a short time of the book's launch. This tactic helps the newly published book rise through sales rankings, ultimately generating greater visibility and increased sales. This book launch strategy isn't the most popular tactic because it can be difficult to coordinate. However, some indie authors have employed this method successfully.

Speaking Gigs

In-person and online speaking gigs are another popular visibility marketing opportunity. This is especially true for authors of expository and inspirational nonfiction whose platforms rely on their ability to instruct or motivate audiences.

In addition to greater visibility and sales, speaking gigs can provide authors with a secondary source of income. For example, I served as a speaker and an affiliate for two of Daniel David Wallace's online writing conferences in 2021. These affiliate opportunities allowed me to earn extra income while introducing my nonfiction work to new writers, adding over 100 subscribers to my email list, and building additional credibility as an authority in the online writing world. Nonfiction authors can enjoy similar opportunities by speaking at online and in-person conferences in their fields. Some may even find success by serving as guest speakers at universities or corporations, depending on the nature of their work.

Fiction authors can also benefit from speaking gigs under the right circumstances. Notable novelists may be invited to speak at online or in-person literary conferences, while others might enjoy the opportunity to speak at local schools or libraries. Novelists are less likely to be paid (or paid well) for speaking gigs, since they aren't teaching or inspiring in a lucrative field (e.g., business, health, and well-being). However, they can still benefit from a boost in book sales and visibility. Some speaking gigs, such as speaking to schoolchildren, can also be personally fulfilling.

Traditional Media

Before the internet, authors pursued visibility marketing opportunities by appearing on television and radio shows, as well as seeking publicity in newspapers and magazines. These opportunities are less popular today since online visibility marketing is much more effective. Most authors find it easier to reach new readers by collaborating with another author than by pitching their book to radio listeners who may or may not read at all. Indie authors also tend to forgo traditional media opportunities because they often require a publicist, which few are willing to employ given the low rate of return.

All this being said, some indie authors enjoy seeking local press opportunities that allow them to connect with their community. Local press outlets rarely require a publicist and may lead to other opportunities to build visibility and credibility, such as a local speaking gig or an invitation to submit your book for a regional award.

Your Social Media Presence

Most authors don't think of their personal social media accounts as a form of visibility marketing, and I won't argue: the nature of running an Instagram account or Facebook author page doesn't fit the definition for visibility marketing that I provided at the top of this chapter. As I previously mentioned, there are many ways to collaborate with other creatives on social platforms. However, there usually isn't any networking involved in posting about your own work on social media. So why am I calling attention to your social presence now?

Here's a hard truth that every author must accept: At the end of the day, your social media presence is out of your control.

At any moment, a social network can change its policies, ban your account, or rework its algorithm—and in doing so, it can decimate your audience and reach. Take Instagram, for example. On June 30, 2021, Adam Mosseri, the head of Instagram, publicly announced that the platform was "no longer just a square photo-sharing app." Instead, Instagram was shifting its focus toward video entertainment content to compete with YouTube and TikTok. In the months that followed, anecdotal evidence suggested that users with Instagram business accounts experienced a marked decline in the growth of their followings when only sharing photos. Meanwhile, users who shifted their focus toward creating Reels—a short style of Instagram video—reported greater reach and growth.

Imagine spending years growing a following on Instagram because you love taking photos and writing engaging captions to connect with your followers. Sure, you can still post photos in the wake of this change, but you'll likely have a much harder time continuing to develop your platform on this app unless you create a video content plan. But what if videography isn't something you enjoy? See how devastating it can be to rely solely on social media as the primary platform for your creative work. There are certainly opportunities for authors to reach more readers and promote their books on social networks, but don't make the mistake of neglecting other platform cornerstones and marketing strategies. Establish your author website, build your email list, and play around with paid advertising— and remember to network with fellow creatives through a few mutually beneficial collaborations.

All this being said, the relatively fickle nature of social networks is why I consider most social media work to be both content marketing and visibility marketing. Yes, you can use social media to build a secondary body of work. However, a social presence is also a mutually beneficial collaboration between you and your network of choice. You benefit by reaching readers and promoting your work on the network, and the network benefits by showing ads in between all the engaging free content you create. See how that works?

As an author, you can use social media in many ways. In addition to posting high-value content, you can run paid ads on social networks, encourage your following to join your email list, and share links to your published books. However, one of the best ways to develop visibility through social media is by "building in public."

Remember that readers can't buy a book if they don't know it exists. They're also far more likely to buy a book when it's been promoted to them repeatedly. Sometimes this promotion is overt. For instance, an author pitches their latest book in an email to their subscribers, then runs a paid Facebook ad promoting the same book to users who subscribe to their email list. Other times, promotion can come in the form of subtle, repeated exposure. A good example of this is when a reader follows an author's progress on social media as they draft, revise, and produce the next book in their self-published fantasy series. By the time that book launches, the reader has formed a deep connection with both the author and the book, so they can't wait to get their hands on a copy.

This is what it means to build in public: to share all the highs and lows of a book's creation long before it ever debuts. You do this by updating readers on your progress, sharing snippets from the manuscript, or regaling readers with a tale from your research process or your final dash to meet a deadline. By allowing your book to take up space in readers' minds, you'll not only give readers an exciting and exclusive peek behind the curtain. You'll also encourage them to connect with your creative work in a way that makes them more likely to purchase, share, and come back for more.

As soon as I knew that I wanted to transform what I'd

intended to be a PDF guide on self-publishing into a full-length book, I began using social media and email to "build" this book in public about nine months before its launch. If you're now reading *Self-Publishing Simplified* because of my visibility marketing efforts, allow me to extend a word of gratitude. It was a pleasure to share my writing and publishing journey with you, and I can't thank you enough for your support along the way.

A Quick-Start Guide to Pitching Successful Collaborations

To take advantage of visibility marketing opportunities, there's a good chance you'll need to pitch to the creators you'd like to collaborate with. To pursue the best possible opportunities and craft high-converting pitches, bear the following four tips in mind.

Tip 1: Consider Pitch Opportunities Wisely

There's little point in collaborating with a creator whose audience doesn't include your ideal reader. Remember that the point of visibility marketing is to develop your reach and introduce your books to new readers who are likely to love your work. So before pursuing any visibility marketing opportunities, always ask yourself whether it will help you engage your ideal readers—or at least a portion of them. For example, you may successfully expand your reach by appearing on a podcast for writers because most writers are also readers. Some of the writers who tune in to the podcast may read within your genre. Others may write in the same niche, which can open up additional collaboration opportunities.

When determining which creators you'll pitch to, also consider the longevity of their platforms. In the early days of running Well-Storied (then She's Novel), I wrote several guest posts for new sites that unfortunately didn't last for more than a year. Those opportunities afforded my site a touch of visibility in the short term, but I ultimately missed out on the additional long-term reach those collaborations could have provided if the sites had stuck around.

To avoid this situation, consider pitching to creators who have maintained their platforms for longer than a year—or who run their platforms as a full-time business. Indie author and podcaster Sacha Black once remarked during an online writing conference that as a general rule of thumb, she only accepts podcast invitations if the show has more than two dozen episodes. Consider creating your own boundaries to ensure the best possible visibility marketing experience.

Finally, consider the size of your audience when pitching to creators. If you're a small-time business blogger who's just published their debut book, the likelihood that Tim Ferriss will welcome you onto his podcast is slim to none. The collaboration wouldn't be mutually beneficial. However, you'll have plenty to offer a creator whose audience is a similar size to yours. Note that I said *similar* rather than *the same*. It's OK to pitch to creators who are slightly out of your league, so to speak. Just remember to be reasonable. You won't curry any favor with well-established creators if you have nothing to offer them in return.

Tip 2: Seek and Follow a Creator's Submission Guidelines

Most creators who run platforms that regularly host guests will have clear submission guidelines on their websites, and they're unlikely to consider pitches that don't follow these rules and boundaries. For example, when I used to accept unsolicited guest posts for publication on the Well-Storied blog, I included an easy link to submission guidelines on my website. These guidelines informed writers what I expected from the content they submitted. If a submission failed to meet those guidelines, I would delete it without responding. My intent wasn't to be rude—I simply didn't want to spend time officially rejecting submissions from writers who didn't care about reading my guidelines.

Remember that the best collaborations are founded on mutual respect. Show other creators that you respect their time and effort by meeting the expectations they outline, and you'll greatly increase your chances of successfully securing a collaboration.

Tip 3: Connect before Pitching a Collaboration

Sometimes cold pitching a creator you haven't interacted with before can be successful. But in most cases, receiving an email from a stranger who suddenly wants the privilege of appearing on your platform can be jarring. Most creators want to engage in collaborations that can lead to ongoing business relationships. If you aren't careful, cold pitching can indicate to a creator that you're not as interested in building a working relationship with them as you are in simply reaping the benefits of the creator's reach.

Whenever possible, take the time to build a relationship with a creator before reaching out. Share their work on social media, comment on their posts, or send them an email to say how much you enjoyed their latest resource. Spend a few weeks interacting with their content before pitching a collaboration, and you'll be far more likely to receive a positive reply.

Tip 4: Personalize Your Pitch

When the time comes to pitch to a creator, craft your email with care. Show the creator that you respect their work by personalizing your pitch. Don't just make a point of including their name once or twice throughout the email. Instead, use a "first me, now you" approach.

First, share why you value the creator's work. Tell them how you've personally benefited from the content they create, and be specific. Perhaps you enjoyed their podcast episode on crafting historically accurate romance novels or their free email course on writing spectacular sales pages. Include a detail in your praise that illustrates that you actually consumed the content and aren't just spinning stories in a poor attempt at flattery.

Then, after telling the creator why you find their content valuable, make your pitch by sharing how *you* can offer value to *their* audience in return. Introduce the creator to your work, and tell them how your experience or expertise can benefit their audience. Perhaps your history as an indie author with a full-time day job and young children has taught you how to balance writing and a busy lifestyle, and you'd like to share those insights with a creator who teaches the writing craft. That's exactly how author M.J. McGriff pitched her article "How to Write a Novel When You Have a Full-Time Life" for publication on the Well-Storied blog in 2017, and I still share that article with my audience to this day. My experience as a full-time creative with no dependents simply can't match M.J.'s insights on this topic.

Following Up on Pitches

After submitting your pitch, give the creator a few days to respond. If, after a week, you still haven't received a reply from them, consider following up with care. Don't assume that the creator is ignoring your email. Most well-established content creators receive dozens (if not hundreds) of emails a day, many of them being pitches of different kinds, so be kind and considerate. Let the creator know that you value the opportunity to work with them but would like to know whether they're not interested in collaborating at this time so you can pursue other opportunities. If you still don't receive a reply after several days, consider moving on. Opportunities to reach new readers abound. Sometimes you simply have to do a little digging to find the collaborations that are most likely to benefit everyone involved.

20

SPIKE MARKETING: BOOK LAUNCHES, RELAUNCHES, AND PRICE DROPS

Here's a truth you might be surprised to learn: book launches are largely overrated.

Many indie authors believe that a book's launch week can make or break its success. This misconception comes from a bygone era in the traditional publishing industry. Because physical bookstores only shelve new books for a matter of weeks, publishers previously poured the bulk of their budgets into marketing new titles. During that period, publishers would make—or fail to make—a return on their investment, and sales determined whether a bookstore would continue to stock a particular book. In most cases, they didn't. The few books that sold phenomenally well during their launch week would continue to get shelf space, which ensured that they would sell well for a longer period simply because they were still available for purchase.

The internet has since leveled the playing field for many traditionally published authors. Books can remain permanently available for sale via online book marketplaces, which has led to greater stability and additional growth opportunities. However, one result of the bygone era is the false belief that a phenomenal launch is key to ongoing success—and, worse yet, that if a book doesn't rocket up the sales rankings during its launch week, it's permanently bound for financial doom. This is nonsense, writer. Online book marketplaces have unlimited shelf space with no turnover dates, which means that readers can find your backlist books just as easily as your latest release.

Book launches can help spike sales for a limited time, but there's no getting around the fact that a book will slowly lose its debut ranking over time. Additional spike marketing tactics can boost its ranking again for another period, but a book won't continue to sell phenomenally just because of your initial book launch marketing efforts. If you want to achieve sustained book sales, long-term marketing efforts—which were covered during the last four chapters—are key to your success.

Nevertheless, spike marketing strategies have their place. While the sales ranking you achieve during launch week might not last, it can still be gratifying to celebrate the release of your book with a week or two of big sales. It can also be rewarding to offer limited-time price drops to your audience, especially when they're paired with some of the paid advertising opportunities discussed in chapter 18. With that in mind, let's explore the most common spike marketing strategies.

Book Launch Marketing Strategies for Beginners

It's difficult to spike your book sales through special promotions such as book launches if you haven't developed an engaged readership yet. That's why debut indie authors who lack an established author platform shouldn't worry about figuring out launch strategies. Instead, they should focus on building the cornerstones of their platform: their author website, email list, social presence, and backlist.

If you're starting completely from scratch, you can employ a few tactics to begin generating book sales. The first is listing your e-book for free. Yes, this might sound ridiculous. You've just spent all this time writing and publishing a book, perhaps even with the intent to kick-start a creative career, and now I'm recommending that you list it for free? It's true, and here's why: The few readers who stumble upon your book despite its low sales ranking aren't likely to purchase a book with no ratings or reviews. The lack of social proof is a major red flag to readers— but it can be overlooked if you remove the financial barrier to entry. By listing your book for free, you'll encourage more readers to give your book a try even without the encouragement of a few five-star ratings.

If you're not sure you can stomach this option, consider enrolling your e-book in KU, where readers can access it for free. You'll still get paid based on the number of pages read, and your book will still be listed for purchase. However, you'll remove the barrier to entry for the large subset of readers who use KU. Just remember that you can't enroll your book in KU without publishing exclusively with Amazon, as discussed in chapter 11.

In either case, you should also make a point of giving away digital copies of your book for free on social media, as well as through your website and newsletter. Create a post that invites new social media followers to message you for a free digital copy, or consider offering your debut book as an incentive for readers to sign up for your email list. If you give content marketing a try, why not announce via your blog posts or podcast episodes that you're giving away free copies of your book? And if you have the opportunity to write a guest post on another author's site, include a link to your free book in your author bio. You can use the BookFunnel app to make distributing free digital copies a cinch.

The best thing you can do as a debut author with no platform, no sales, and no reviews is get your book out there. Make your book as visible and accessible as possible so you can start generating early ratings and reviews. Generosity promotes this mission, while cost inhibits it. So give freely, and readers will put some wind beneath your wings. But don't give at all, and you won't just start from the ground up; you'll stay there.

Preparing for a Successful Book Launch

If you've established your author platform and developed a notable readership—say, at least 100 email subscribers—there are two primary launch strategies you can employ to spike your book sales shortly after its release. Spiking your sales will increase your book's initial sales ranking, making the book more visible to potential readers who are scrolling through online book marketplaces. Depending on the size of your existing readership, these strategies may even help your book earn best-seller status on Amazon. For example, when I launched *Build Your Best Writing Life* to my list of 10,000 subscribers on January 2, 2020, the book became the number one best seller in the "Authorship" category on Amazon. Any reader who clicked on the book's listing would have seen the orange tag denoting its best-seller status, which likely helped boost sales to some degree. That "best seller" tag only lasted a few days before another took the top spot, but it was nevertheless the cherry on top of my launch experience.

So what are the two main strategies that can help your book rocket through the sales rankings on release day?

Strategy 1: Run a Preorder Campaign

A **preorder campaign** allows readers to purchase your book before launch day. However, they won't receive the book until or after the day of its release, just as you won't receive any royalties until or after that day. So what's the point of running a preorder campaign?

First, a preorder campaign can help build excitement for your book. If your existing readership is full of your book's ideal readers, there's a good chance they're already eagerly awaiting your book's release. Offering the book for preorder ramps up anticipation and encourages them to buy it. A preorder campaign is also a great way to begin marketing your book with the intent to sell (rather than simply building its visibility). Remember that many readers won't purchase your book the first time you pitch it to them. They may be busy, between paychecks, or simply unconvinced that your book is worth their time and money. Repeated exposure, however, will help convince many of those readers to eventually buy it. Running a preorder campaign is a great way to begin exposing your upcoming release to your established readership.

Additionally, running a preorder campaign can spike sales on release day if you're purposefully trying to hit a best-seller list. However, this involves some clarification. When running a preorder campaign through Amazon KDP, preorders help your book climb sales rankings *before* release day, allowing readers who aren't already part of your readership to discover and preorder your book through Amazon. However, preorder sales aren't actually *reported* as sales until your release date. This means that you won't officially earn royalties until your book launches. It also means that your reported sales will spike on release day to account for all the preorders you sold—a spike that, under the right circumstances, might help you hit the *New York Times* or *USA Today* best-seller lists. Indie authors seeking those bragging rights often combine a robust preorder campaign with other marketing strategies we've discussed (e.g., paid ads, visibility marketing) to increase their chances of hitting a list during the early days of their book's release.

If you'd like to run a preorder campaign, there are a couple of important things to know. First, nearly all e-book distributors allow preorder campaigns. You can also use IngramSpark to run a preorder campaign for print books. Most distributors allow you to create a preorder campaign at least ninety days in advance of your book's release, if not longer. However, most indie authors opt to run preorder campaigns that last between one and three weeks. Extending your campaign any longer can risk killing the sense of excitement and anticipation that makes preorder campaigns so effective. The book you're selling will then feel too intangible, something that might be forgotten with time.

When creating a preorder campaign, it's important to set a release date you know you can meet. Ideally, your files should be finalized and your listings ready to go. Because once you select a release date, most platforms will penalize you if you fail to have your files ready to submit on the submission deadline (or if you cancel a release altogether). Amazon KDP offers one chance for a delay before revoking your capability to set up a new preorder campaign (or delay existing releases) for an entire year. Repeatedly delaying releases can also breed mistrust with your readership, undercutting their excitement and faith in your credibility. Yikes!

One of the best ways to accrue a large number of preorders is to offer your book at a discounted price before its launch. For example, if you intend to sell your e-book at a regular price of $3.99, you may want to list the e-book on preorder for just $0.99. Offering this discounted preorder price is a great way to spike sales and reward your readership for their early support.

Strategy 2: Build an Advance Reader Team

By running a preorder campaign, you can spike sales leading up to and during launch. More sales lead to a higher sales ranking, which in turn means that your book will be visible to more readers who are searching for their next great read in their online marketplace of choice. Unfortunately, many readers won't take a chance on a new book or author without social proof. They want to see ratings and reviews that can help them determine whether your book is worth buying. If you've run a preorder campaign as your sole book launch marketing strategy, your book won't have any ratings or reviews—and you might miss out on valuable sales in the early days of your book's publication.

So how do you solve this problem? This is where an advance reader team, or street team, comes into play.

An **advance reader team** is a subsection of your existing readership (namely a subsection of your email list subscribers) who receive an early copy of your book—also known as an advance review copy or ARC—for free in exchange for leaving an honest public rating and review on Amazon, Goodreads, or another book-related platform. You can build this team through your email list simply by inviting readers to join. And when the time comes to deliver the free digital copy, consider using BookFunnel to make distribution easy. As I mentioned during chapter 17, the BookFunnel team will take care of all technical difficulties and customer service for you.

Before sending out ARCs, it's important to note that Amazon's customer product review policy doesn't allow sellers to compensate customers for reviews in any way. So when you send ARCs to your advance reader team, remind them that they aren't legally obligated to leave a review on your book's listing. It's ultimately their decision whether they'll honor the intent of the agreement. Also, encourage your team to use disclaimers when reviewing your book. Here's one such example: "I received a free copy of this book without obligation to leave a review. The following opinions are my own." This disclaimer will discourage Amazon from accidentally removing reviews that don't violate their terms and conditions.

NOTE: Some indie authors offer ARCs to readers through NetGalley, a website that connects authors with early readers who are willing to leave reviews. This is a great option for authors who haven't yet built a robust email list of subscribers willing to join their advance reader team.

To generate ratings and reviews before release day, many indie authors do a **soft launch** (i.e., a restricted release) of their book. Running a soft launch is easy. Simply make your book available for sale a few days before your intended launch date —that is, the day when you'll publicly announce the launch of your book to your readership. During these few days between your book's soft launch and actual launch, email your ARC team to let them know it's time to leave their reviews. You may also want to ask them to purchase a steeply discounted copy of your e-book *before* leaving a review on Amazon, since purchasing the book first will cause their review to be marked as "verified." Anecdotal evidence suggests that verified reviews hold greater weight within the Amazon algorithm, which means they'll help your book achieve greater visibility in that marketplace.

While I chose to focus on this second strategy when launching *Build Your Best Writing Life*, there's no reason you can't combine a preorder campaign with the power of early reviews. The trick is to work out how and when you'll ask your advance reader team to leave their reviews. On Amazon, readers can't leave reviews for a book that's available for preorder, even if they've received an ARC. So you can encourage your advance reader team to leave reviews on the day your book launches, or you can be a little sneaky and publish the paperback version of your book before the release of your e-book. This will allow your advance reader team to leave reviews on the paperback edition while your preorder campaign is still active. Those reviews will show up on your e-book listing, just as e-book reviews will be visible on your paperback listing. The only downside is that you can't discount a paperback edition as steeply for your advance reader team as you can an e-book. Nevertheless, early ratings and reviews, even unverified, can give your book listing the social proof it needs to encourage new readers to buy your book as it soars up the charts.

Crafting Your Book Launch Plan

When it comes to planning your book launch, getting started early is key. Book launch and prelaunch marketing strategies take time to coordinate, especially if you're working with an advance reader team or planning a book blog tour. The last thing you want to do is layer extra stress on top of last-minute launch tasks such as finalizing your book's listing and reviewing preview copies for formatting mistakes. Give everyone who's involved in your book's launch some breathing room (yourself included), and you'll ensure an enjoyable release experience that early readers and visibility collaborators (and you!) won't mind repeating.

Regardless of whether you work with an advance reader team, you may want to soft-launch your book anyway to give yourself a few days to confirm that all is well with your book's listing (e.g., the description formatting renders correctly, the pricing is correct). You can also use this time to claim your book on Amazon Author Central so that it's linked to your author name. This guarantees that your book will show up under your public author profile on Amazon. Other tasks you can complete during your book's soft launch include requesting to add your book to additional Amazon categories (which we discussed in chapter 12) and adding listing links to your website, BookBub profile, and Goodreads account.

And here's a bonus tip: You can use a tool called Geniuslink to create a single URL that automatically redirects readers to their preferred Amazon marketplace when clicked (e.g., Amazon.com, Amazon.co.uk). This simplifies the shopping experience for international readers, decreasing the chances that they'll click away from your book's listing before purchasing it.

On the day of your book's actual launch, drive traffic to your sales pages using some of the marketing strategies we've discussed throughout part 3. For instance, you can send a launch announcement to your email list, post about your book's release on social media, or create a special blog post, podcast episode, or YouTube video celebrating your book launch. You can also run a paid ad or two on your platform(s) of choice or coordinate a few last-minute collaborations with fellow creatives to pitch your book to a wider audience. Use whichever options best fit your schedule and help you connect with your ideal readers.

Finally, remember to celebrate the release of your book. Some authors enjoy hosting in-person book launch parties. Such parties often require a lot of time and money to coordinate, and most authors report that launch parties have little impact on their sales and reach. Nevertheless, hosting a party for your family, friends, and community can be a fun way to celebrate your creative accomplishment. Alternatively, consider hosting an online book launch party via a social media live event or webinar. Or, if you're an extreme introvert like me, treat yourself to a fancy dinner, a slice of cake, or a good book. The choice is up to you! The point, of course, is to take a moment to revel in the joy of all you've accomplished. Writing a book isn't easy, and neither is producing and publishing it. By taking these steps, you've made incredible progress toward achieving your personal definition of publishing success.

Spiking Sales with Price Drops

Many authors try to boost sales of their backlist books by running occasional **price drops** (i.e., discounting the book for a limited time). This strategy can be a great way to thank your readership for their support and encourage them to purchase your book if they haven't done so yet. This is especially true for readers who enjoy purchasing books when they're on sale to make their reading habit more affordable.

Spiking sales with a price drop can also increase your book's visibility, helping an older title reach new readers. To increase the sales spike your book experiences, consider running a sale during applicable peak seasons. Think of promoting self-help books after New Year's, romance during February, and horror around Halloween. You can also host price drops to celebrate the anniversary of a book's release or a milestone in your publishing journey.

One of the best ways to maximize a price drop is to promote the sale with paid ads. Be sure to review chapter 18 if you plan to discount your book anytime soon. Also, while some platforms allow you to schedule price changes, many (including Amazon) require you to alter the price of your book manually. Make sure you do this a few days before promoting the price drop, as it may take up to seventy-two hours for the new price to go public.

Updating and Relaunching Older Books

Sometimes indie authors don't produce the highest quality books when they kick-start their publishing journeys. Maybe they had a small production budget and didn't invest in freelance editing or a great book cover. Maybe inexperience led them to publish a book that lacked strong structure or prose. Or maybe they chose a title that failed to effectively market their book or realized that they'd prefer to republish an older book under a new pen name.

Whatever the case, the wonderful thing about self-publishing is that indie authors have full control over the production of their books at all times. This means that you can alter and reupload books in your backlist to meet your current standards or marketing goals. Doing so can have a positive impact on book sales, the reading experience, and your overall success as an indie author. You can even use a relaunch to spike sales using the same strategies you used with a book's initial release!

If you'd like to relaunch an older book, do so with care. Making numerous changes to your book over time can lead to reader confusion, so make all of your desired changes during a single relaunch if possible. What exactly should that relaunch look like? Well, that depends on the changes you've made. Let's look at a few examples of changes you might want to make to your book.

Fixing Typos

Reuploading an interior book file to fix typos isn't considered a relaunch. As long as you haven't added or removed major sections of content, you don't need to make any changes to your listing, denote the new file as a second edition, or announce the newly uploaded file to your readership. You also don't need to list the new interior file under a new ISBN.

Uploading a New Cover

If you'd like to update your cover but don't intend to change your book's title or your author name, you don't need to create a new listing for your book or apply a new ISBN. However, if you're changing your cover in a way that substantially changes readers' perceptions of your book (e.g., a sweet romance cover to an erotica cover), consider creating a new book listing and using a new ISBN to avoid customer complaints.

Changing a Title or Author Name

If you're switching up your book's title, subtitle, or author name, your book will be considered a new edition. You'll need to create a new listing for your book and use a new ISBN, which means that you will lose ratings and reviews from the old edition of your book. To retain that social proof, contact the distributor's customer service team to get the ratings and reviews to carry over. When dealing with Amazon, note your book's original Amazon Standard Identification Number (ASIN). This identifier is different from your book's ISBN. You can then contact Amazon to request that they apply your old ASIN to your new book listing, which will preserve your existing ratings and reviews.

When changing your book's title or author name, you'll need to upload a new cover that features the appropriate information. It's also a good idea to include a note in your book's listing description that tells readers the book was previously published under a different title or author name. This will prevent readers from accidentally purchasing the same book twice, which can potentially lead to negative reviews.

When you change your book's title or author name but not the content of the book, you can choose whether to officially relaunch the book using the spike marketing tactics discussed in this chapter. But at the very least, let your existing audience know about the change.

Releasing a Revised Edition

A book is considered a revised edition if you make minor but notable changes to its content. This can include changing a secondary character's name, removing an inadvertently offensive remark, or updating data based on new scientific studies. As long as changes are kept to a minimum (less than 10 percent of the book's word count is a good rule of thumb) and don't impact the book's content in a way that would alter its listing description, you can simply reupload your new interior file via your existing listing. However, you may want to include a quick revision disclaimer in your book's listing description for added clarity and transparency.

Releasing a New Edition

If you've overhauled the content of your book in a major way, such as changing at least 10 percent of the book's content or rewriting the book in a way that would impact its listing description, you'll need to reupload your book as a second edition (or third, fourth, etc.). This means that you'll need to create a new listing and use a new ISBN. However, if your new edition features the same book title and author name, you can use the method outlined in the "Changing a Title or Author Name" section above to ensure that your ratings and reviews carry over.

That being said, if you're changing the content of your book to the point that it's no longer the same book (e.g., you've radically improved its plot or structure), you may not want the old ratings and reviews to carry over. If they do appear on your new listing because you're using the same title and author name, contact Amazon's customer service team to request that a new ASIN be applied to the current edition of your book. This should remove any old ratings and reviews from your current listing.

Finally, any time you release a new edition of your book, consider employing some of the book launch marketing strategies we've already discussed in this book. In essence, you've written and published a new book. So make sure to share your accomplishment loudly and proudly—and enjoy a spike in sales while you're at it!

21

MARKETING STRATEGIES FOR LONG-TERM GROWTH

I n *How to Market a Book*, six-figure indie author Joanna Penn says this: "Strategy is deciding what you want to do, and perhaps more importantly, what you *don't* want to do."

Some of the marketing strategies discussed over the last few chapters can help you spike your book's sales and visibility for a short period. Others can help you slowly but surely build a thriving readership and a full-time income as a self-published author. In many ways, spike marketing strategies feed into this long-term growth. A reader who discovers and purchases one of your books during launch or a limited-time price drop might go on to join your email list, purchase more of your books, and leave fantastic ratings and reviews on your listings. These are just some of the actions that can not only establish this reader as a long-term member of your readership but also help you expand the reach of your author platform.

All this being said, there's more than one right approach to book marketing—and no two successful indie authors will approach book marketing in the same way. We all write different books for different ideal readers, publish on different schedules, and have different marketing budgets and capacities. We also have interests and preferences that lead us to maintain certain strategies over others. With that in mind, how do you know which book marketing strategies are right for you —and, on the flip side, which ones aren't?

Ultimately, the methods that will help you best reach more readers and sell more books will meet these two key criteria.

Criterion 1: The Best Marketing Strategies Are Effective

There's nothing strategic about employing marketing methods that don't help you effectively get your books into the hands of your ideal readers. The same goes for marketing methods that don't help you achieve your personal definition of publishing success. For example, if you write literary fiction, you'll struggle to market your books through book promotion sites that cater to genre fiction readers. Likewise, if your goal is to publish a large number of books per year, you'll struggle to maintain time-consuming content marketing efforts.

If you want to effectively market your books for long-term growth, you'll need clarity about your creative niche, your preferred author business model, and your goals for your publishing experience. The more you understand these elements, the more quickly you'll understand which marketing methods will—and won't—effectively serve your audience and mission.

In chapter 14, we explored the push-versus-pull marketing spectrum. Some authors favor one extreme, relying solely on paid advertising or community-building efforts to build their readerships and sell their books. If you feel one extreme calling your name, go ahead and explore it. However, most successful indie authors fall somewhere in the middle of this spectrum, using both push and pull marketing tactics to some degree. The same indie authors cultivate a thorough understanding of a broad range of marketing strategies and develop the skills to execute on each one with notable success.

If the thought of replicating such success feels overwhelming, take a step back and breathe. Yes, it takes time and effort to research, understand, and implement new marketing strategies. It's also true that most strategies involve months—if not years—of testing and honing before you see exciting results. And after all that time and effort, there's still the possibility that some strategies won't be effective. The fact that you're in this for the long haul is your saving grace.

If you've adopted the indie author mindset, then you aren't looking for immediate results. You understand that most successful indie authors spend years building their readerships and revenue from the ground up, and you're willing to commit to the journey because you know that pursuing a creative career will help you live your fullest, freest, most fulfilling writing life.

With that in mind, remember that you have time. You don't need to implement every marketing strategy under the sun from the second you publish your debut book. In fact, it's best to start as small as possible and stick to the basics. Get your author website up and running, or create your email list and put together a simple incentive and welcome sequence. Establishing the cornerstones of your author platform will help you lay the foundation for your additional book marketing efforts, which you should explore with patience and focus. If you put too many irons in the fire, you're bound to get burned. Instead, choose one or two strategies that you believe will most effectively help you reach the early members of your readership, then commit to exploring and experimenting with those tactics for several months.

If you're new to publishing for profit, remember that spike marketing strategies won't be effective until you've built a readership and established relevance with paid advertising networks. It also takes time to hone your voice and skill as a content and email marketer. The same goes for developing strong connections and effective collaborations when engaging in visibility marketing. So be patient. Don't be afraid to test, tweak, or change your approach to any marketing strategies as needed. Reiterate often. Ask yourself what isn't working, how you can fix it, and how you can continue to improve and develop your skills. Approach book marketing as an explorer and a scientist, and you'll soon learn how to effectively market your books for big-time, long-term success.

Criterion 2: The Best Marketing Strategies Are Sustainable

It can be incredibly rewarding to boost the reach and revenue of your books. But if you loathe the marketing strategies you've put into practice, you probably won't sustain them for long. That's why the best book marketing strategies are the ones you enjoy—or, at the very least, the ones you don't mind maintaining.

By this point, you should have an inkling as to which marketing strategies appeal to you. Explore these strategies first as long as you believe they'll help you effectively boost your reach and revenue. However, over the long term, don't avoid exploring popular marketing strategies simply because you don't believe you'll like them. Many methods only seem off-putting until you understand their ins and outs, while others may surprise you. I've grown to love using Instagram to connect with my readership even though I'm not the biggest fan of being in front of the camera. The heartfelt conversations and deep connections I've built there never fail to put a smile on my face.

Alternatively, you may uncover effective marketing strategies you're willing to maintain even though you're not overjoyed about the work. Don't shy away from these tactics. No one

—including a self-employed creative—loves every aspect of their career. As long as you don't find yourself avoiding a particular marketing strategy out of sheer loathing, it's likely worth maintaining.

Finally, please know that it's OK to operate differently than other indie authors. Don't hesitate to forgo book marketing strategies you don't enjoy, even if it seems like everyone else is doing them. There's little point in turning your new creative career into yet another soul-sucking day job. That's why you'll rarely see me do live content online. Webinars and social media live events may be widely effective marketing strategies, but I'm an anxiety-prone introvert. The least sustainable way for me to market my creative work would be to throw all my energy at a live event that would send my nervous system into overdrive for days. Just because you choose to do things differently doesn't mean you're doing anything wrong. You do you, author.

By extension, the best book marketing strategies are the ones that fit into your schedule and don't steal unnecessary time and energy from your writing efforts. There's no getting around the fact that all authors must market their books to make a living. Promotion requires time and effort, but the way you approach this responsibility is yours to decide.

Most indie authors spend a small amount of time on marketing each day or week. However, some indie authors block off larger amounts of time to promote their books. They may devote one week per month to their marketing efforts, setting their writing projects aside to focus entirely on frontloading and scheduling as much marketing content as possible. Or they may switch between writing and marketing every few months to focus on the task at hand.

The authors who employ these latter methods are few and far between. Most are novelists who find it difficult to switch between storytelling and marketing on a daily or weekly basis. If this concept appeals to you, then by all means give it a try.

The choice is yours, and you can always switch approaches if you find that one isn't working out. A little flexibility is key to sustained efforts, including book marketing.

Putting Effective, Sustainable Marketing into Practice

By determining which marketing tactics are both effective and sustainable for you, you'll discover which book promotion strategies will be integral to your long-term growth and success as an indie author.

As you gain experience during your publishing journey, avoid getting stuck in your ways. Remember what I mentioned a moment ago: a little flexibility is key to sustained efforts. As the internet and other technologies evolve alongside the indie publishing industry, your most effective and sustainable marketing strategies will evolve with them. Just as a paid advertising campaign can make a killing one month and then be less successful the next month, there will undoubtedly be book promotion strategies that won't stand the test of time. Be mindful of the tactics that no longer serve your audience and your work, and be willing to explore new methods over time. Keep an open mind, and give yourself permission to tinker and explore. The greater your intrepid spirit, the more enduring your success as an indie author will be.

Finally, remember that the beautiful thing about building a career as an indie author is that your efforts compound. One book sale leads to more. A great review can convince multiple readers to buy your book. The visibility of your work expands to a greater and greater magnitude with more word-of-mouth recommendations and online social shares. And the work you do today? It doesn't just earn you a paycheck tomorrow. It can also provide income for the rest of your life. With every book you write, you can generate multiple streams of income you can profit from until the day you die—and your loved ones can benefit financially, too, until your book enters the public domain about seventy years after your death.

By self-publishing, you're not only cultivating an exciting and fulfilling creative career or publishing journey. You're also building a legacy that readers and loved ones alike can cherish for years to come. So what are you waiting for, author? It's time to write, publish, and profit from your creative work!

CONCLUSION

If I could go back in time and impart one message to myself when I was just beginning my writing journey, it would be this: Difficult creative work doesn't have to be draining. Indeed, there's incredible reward to be found in challenge.

By finishing this book, you've likely gained far more knowledge about the self-publishing process than you had when you began. Nevertheless, you may be feeling overwhelmed. Self-publishing a profitable book is a mammoth endeavor. The information in this book is meant to help simplify the process by acting as a handy reference guide, but the fact is that very little about the indie author journey is easy. It takes immense time and effort to write a book and an equal dose of emotional resilience to seek the feedback needed to polish it to a high shine. From there, producing and publishing a book requires diligence, know-how, and considerable financial investment. Successfully attracting the readers who are most likely to love your book further necessitates marketing savvy and an intrepid creative spirit.

If you're committed to this journey despite its many trials, take a moment to marvel at your courage. You need audacity to

diverge from the status quo in search of deep creative fulfillment, and that's the path you've chosen. Be proud of that decision. Revel in it for a short while, then take care to mind the
path ahead.

Your self-publishing journey will include steep climbs,
rocky passes, and unexpected storms. Readers will rate your
books poorly. You'll struggle to move the needle on book sales.
You might even wonder if all the time and effort you've poured
into developing your platform is really worth it. This isn't to say
that your self-publishing journey will be nothing but doom and
gloom, but it's important to remember that the path before you
isn't a paved road from rags to riches. The key to weathering
difficulties in your self-publishing journey—and, ultimately,
achieving all you desire for your writing life—is calling upon
your indie author mindset. With this in mind, let's revisit the
five essential mental models discussed in part I.

Mental Model 1: Commitment Is Key

Indie authors take responsibility for their creative successes,
treating their work with the same level of respect and professionalism as one would in any other career. They recognize that
motivation is most often the *result* of action rather than the
cause of it, and they employ strong work habits to cultivate
momentum in their writing lives.

Mental Model 2: Failure Is a Launchpad

Successful indie authors recognize that at various points in
their publishing journeys, they'll experience what others might
perceive as failures. However, they don't view these incidents as
losses. Instead, they treat perceived failures as valuable
learning experiences, actively gleaning lessons and insights
they can harness to redirect their efforts for the better.

Mental Model 3: Doubt Is a Springboard

Successful indie authors don't treat doubt as an obstacle to overcome or a weakness to suppress. Instead, they recognize that doubt indicates potential issues in their writing lives, and they work intentionally to identify and resolve these issues as soon as possible. This mindful approach helps them harness doubt as a springboard for creative growth.

Mental Model 4: Fortune Favors the Enterprising

Successful indie authors understand that the platform development and book marketing strategies they currently employ might become less effective over time, so they take proactive action to ensure their continued success. They study industry trends and changes, explore new marketing efforts, and make a point of learning the ins and outs of new technologies that might impact their creative work.

Mental Model 5: The Journey Is the Reward

Successful indie authors don't view their goals as destinations they must reach before they can find joy and fulfillment in their writing lives. Instead, they reject their egos and use their goals as guideposts, reveling in everyday challenges and accomplishments as they enjoy every step of their publishing journey.

It's Time for Your Self-Publishing Journey to Begin

There are plenty of challenges in self-publishing a profitable book, and tackling the self-publishing learning curve itself can be an intimidating creative endeavor. But very few pains in life are as terrible as the one caused by ignoring a creative calling.

By choosing to self-publish, you're taking brave and powerful action to manifest your writing dreams. You're saying no to *one day* and *if only* and yes to embarking on an exhilarating climb. Refer to this book as often as you need to during your trek. Allow it to guide you through your self-publishing journey one step at a time, and you'll soon experience a creative reward like no other: the incredible pride that comes with publishing profitable books that your readers adore.

Talk about a spectacular view, writer.

GLOSSARY OF TERMS

NOTE: The following terms are defined within the context of independent authorship and book publication. Some terms also have broader definitions not listed in this glossary.

Acquisitions editor: an editor responsible for reviewing unsolicited manuscripts and book proposals in search of works a publishing house can successfully produce and market

Ad spend: the amount of money spent to run an online paid advertisement

Advance reader team: a group of readers an author selects to receive a free, pre-publication copy of their book in exchange for an honest public rating and review on the book's listing page or on social media; also known as a street team

Advance: the set sum of money an author is guaranteed to earn upon selling their book's publication rights to a traditional publisher; often paid out in multiple installments leading up to the book's publication

Advance review copy (ARC): a free copy of a book gifted by an author to a reader before publication in exchange for an honest public rating and review; also known as an advance reading copy

Advertising cost of sale (ACoS): a metric that measures the efficiency of a paid advertisement by determining the percentage of generated sales revenue spent running the ad

Aggregator: an online platform through which an author can create a single book listing to be distributed to multiple marketplaces, library apps, and book subscription services of their choosing

Assisted self-publishing company: a company that shoulders the responsibility of producing all aspects of an author's self-published book for an up-front fee

Audiobook: a digital recording of a reading of a book

Author name: the real or fictional name under which an author publishes their book

Author platform: an author's capacity for generating revenue as determined by the visibility and credibility of their work

Back cover copy: the descriptive copy that appears on the back of a book's print editions

Backlink: an incoming hyperlink from one website to another website

Backlist: the extent of an author's published books available for sale

Beta reader: a reader who provides an author with casual, unpaid feedback on an unpublished manuscript

Bleed: content printed at the edge of a page, such as an illustration

Book blogger: an online influencer who publicly reviews books on their blog or social media account

Book description: the sales text that appears on a book's online sales pages

Branding: the process of developing the features that distinguish one author or imprint from another

Category: a subsection of books in an online marketplace that share key characteristics, which an author can select when creating a listing to help their book find its ideal readers

Click-through rate (CTR): an advertising metric that indicates the percentage of shoppers who click on an ad to learn more about the book

Content marketing: a long-term book promotion strategy that involves building and maintaining an online body of work designed to attract and engage one's ideal readers

Content warning: a cautionary statement included in a book's front matter and listing description that indicates events or language contained within the book that some readers might find triggering

Contributor: a professional collaborator, such as a cowriter or illustrator, who helps cocreate a book

Copyediting: a type of editing that focuses on the consistency and accuracy of the language an author uses in the text

Copyright: a legal right to copy and distribute a creative work

Copywriting: the act of writing text intended to promote an author, book, or imprint

Cover design: the artwork on the outside of a book that aims to attract readers and provide a clear impression of the book's contents

Creative niche: the unique definition of what an author writes and who they write for; also known as a hook

Design brief: a document that lists the information a designer needs to produce a custom book cover design, such as its genre and themes

Developmental editing: a type of editing that focuses on critiquing the structure and content of a written work; also known as content editing or structural editing

Digital proof: a formatted digital copy of a book used for making corrections before publication; also known as a galley

Digital rights management (DRM): a type of access control technology used to restrict the use of copyrighted works, often to prevent illegal sharing

Distributor: an online platform an author can use to list their book for sale in the specific online marketplace(s) the platform serves, such as Amazon or Barnes & Noble

Domain name: a unique web address, which an author may wish to purchase when creating a website for their work

Edition: a particular version of a book

Edition number: a number that indicates a particular version of a book, especially a book that has been revised and republished

Editorial letter: a multipage write-up created by an editor to offer feedback on the content and structure of a manuscript

Email marketing: the act of engaging with one's audience or promoting a published work through email

Email marketing service: a type of email service provider that allows an author to build and contact a list of subscribed readers

EPUB: an e-book file format that uses the .epub file extension and is supported by many e-readers and reading apps

Formatting: the act of preparing the layout of a manuscript for print and digital distribution; also known as interior book design

Freelance editor: a self-employed editor whom authors can contract to complete manuscript editing services

Funnel: a marketing system for transforming potential readers into fans who purchase one or more of an author's books

High-volume publishing: a business model that outlines how an author can earn a living primarily through royalty income by publishing multiple books a year in highly commercial markets

Hook: the unique definition of what an author writes and who they write for; also known as a creative niche

Hybrid author: an author who publishes at least one work traditionally and one work independently

Ideal reader: the specific type of person who is most likely to love an author's books

Impressions: the number of times a paid advertisement is shown to consumers

Imprint: a brand name under which a book is published; also known as a publishing trade name

Independent author: an author who self-publishes a book for profit, especially with the intent to build or maintain a career as a published author

Intellectual property: creative work protected under law from unauthorized use, to which an author owns various legal rights including copyright and publication rights

Interior book design: the act of preparing the layout of a manuscript for print and digital distribution; also known as formatting

International Standard Book Number (ISBN): a unique thirteen-digit identifier that must be assigned to most editions of a published book

Keyword: a word or short phrase added to a book listing's metadata to provide online marketplace algorithms with information about where, when, and to whom a book should be shown

Line editing: a type of editing that focuses on ensuring that an author uses the best possible language to convey their point or tell their story, as well as helping an author refine their writing style

Literary agent: a professional who represents an author in dealings with publishers and press and who may aid an author in the development of their career and creative works

Medium: a form of art; the type of online media or media platform an author uses to build a body of work

Metadata: the secondary data in book listings and author profiles that provide information about your book

Online marketplace: a website that sells books to consumers

Paid advertising: any type of ad that an author can purchase to promote a book or another offering intended to grow their readership

Per-finished-hour (PFH) rate: the flat rate many narrators charge for the recording and engineering of a finished hour of audio, especially in regard to the production of an audiobook

Preorder campaign: a coordinated effort to sell copies of a book before it is available with the understanding that the book will be delivered on or shortly after publication day

Price drop: a discount offered on a book for a limited time

Print-on-demand (POD): a service offered by a book distributor or aggregator through which the company will print and ship physical copies of a book directly to the readers who order them

Printed proof: a printed copy of a formatted book used for making corrections before publication; also known as a galley

Proofreading: the act of ensuring that a printed or digital proof matches the text of a finalized manuscript, contains no remaining errors or inconsistencies, and is formatted correctly for print-on-demand and online distribution; this term may also refer to final corrections made to an author's manuscript before it has been formatted for distribution

Pseudonym: a fictional name used as an author name; a pen name

Publication rights: the exclusive rights to produce and distribute a manuscript, which an author may sell to a publisher for a contracted period of time

Publisher: a company that produces and distributes books for sale; also known as a publishing house

Pull marketing: the act of employing promotion strategies intended to attract and maintain readers' interest in an author's work

Push marketing: the act of employing promotion strategies intended to encourage book sales, website clicks, or email subscriptions

Relevance: a metric determined by the effectiveness of an author's past Amazon Ads campaigns that determines the visibility of the author's latest ad

Royalty: the sum of money an author earns for each sale of their book, which is determined by contracted royalty rates (e.g., 25 percent of list price per unit sold)

Sample edit: a free edit completed by a freelance editor on a small portion of an author's manuscript to help both parties determine whether they wish to collaborate and/or to help the editor determine an appropriate rate for a service

Search engine optimization (SEO): the act of maximizing the number of visitors to a particular site by crafting content designed to appear high in a list of search engine results

Second brain: a term coined by productivity expert Tiago Forte to define a digital system for storing ideas and information

Self-publishing: the act of producing and distributing a book for sale without the aid of a publishing house

Sensitivity reader: a reader who specializes in providing professional feedback that concerns the author's portrayal of a sensitive topic in an unpublished manuscript, as informed by their own lived experience

Soft launch: a restricted release of a book intended to allow an author's advance reader team to leave early ratings and reviews on the book's listings and to allow the author time to check for errors on their book's sales page before a public launch

Spike marketing: the act of employing promotion strategies designed to increase a book's sales revenue and ranking for a limited time

Traditional publishing: the act of selling a manuscript's publication rights to a publishing house for production and distribution

Visibility marketing: the act of employing promotion strategies designed to increase awareness of an author's works

Web host: a company that stores site files on its servers and connects them to the internet for a subscription fee, which an author will need to pay to create a website

Website builder: a platform an author can use to create a website

AUTHOR'S NOTE

This book contains information about self-publishing tools, services, and pricing that is likely to change over time. My intent is to keep this book up-to-date, reviewing its content often and making changes when necessary. Any help in this endeavor is welcome. If you recently purchased a copy of this book and have discovered information you believe to be incorrect, out-of-date, or missing, please feel free to email me at kristen@well-storied.com.

LOOKING FOR MORE?

Thank you for reading *Self-Publishing Simplified*, writer. I hope you not only enjoyed the book but continue to find it useful as a reference guide in your publishing journey. If you've already found it helpful, would you consider rating and reviewing *Self-Publishing Simplified* on Amazon or another online marketplace? As you know from chapter 20, this type of social proof goes a long way toward helping a book reach new readers and thrive.

For further guidance in your publishing journey, you might enjoy *The Ultimate Self-Publishing Toolkit*. This free PDF contains a directory of editing, cover design, formatting, and book distribution services and resources. To download your free copy of *The Ultimate Self-Publishing Toolkit*, visit https:// www.well-storied.com/toolkit.

ACKNOWLEDGMENTS

In chapter 7, I wrote that it takes a village to raise a book. This sentiment undoubtedly holds true for *Self-Publishing Simplified*.

To my early beta readers—Lucas, Erik, Carey, Rubina, Sirine, and Áine—thank you for opening my eyes to this project's full potential. Without your feedback, I wouldn't have given this book permission to spread its wings. To Nora, Lindsey, Sara, Marina, Daniel, Julie, Anatoli, Divine, Kate, AJ, Sarah, Aimee, Tori, Jess, Rona, Lou, Breanna, Anid, and Kelly-Ann, the time and care you invested in this book as part of my second round of beta readers are invaluable. Thank you for helping me guide *Self-Publishing Simplified* into top form.

To my editors, Sara Letourneau and Sarah Kolb-Williams, thank you for helping this book shed its baby fat and find its voice. Working with you is always a joy and a privilege, and your efforts on behalf of this project are appreciated beyond words.

Finally, to the Well-Storied community, thank you for your continued support and readership. It's an honor to serve you in your creative journey and witness all the incredible magic you usher into this world. I can't wait to see what you create next.

ABOUT THE AUTHOR

Kristen Kieffer is an author, podcaster, and writing coach based outside Philadelphia, Pennsylvania. She teaches writers how to confidently and consistently craft stories that connect through her work at Well-Storied, which is frequently voted among top sites for writers. When not putting pen to paper, she can be found with her nose in a book, her feet on a trail, or her hands full of treats for her rescue dog Aggie.

instagram.com/kristen_kieffer

amazon.com/author/kristenkieffer

bookbub.com/authors/kristen-kieffer

Made in the USA
Middletown, DE
06 March 2022